KT-118-812

a Vegetarian Christmas

Rose Elliot

Thorsons

Thorsons
An imprint of HarperCollins*Publishers*
77–85 Fulham Palace Road,
Hammersmith, London W6 8JB

The Thorsons website address is: www.thorsons.com

First published by Thorsons 1992
This edition 2000

10 9 8 7 6

© Rose Elliot 2000

Rose Elliot asserts the moral right to
be identified as the author of this work

A catalogue record for this book
is available from the British Library

ISBN 0 00 710130 9

Printed and bound in Great Britain by
Martins the Printers Limited,
Berwick upon Tweed

All rights reserved. No part of this publication may be
reproduced, stored in a retrieval system, or transmitted,
in any form or by any means, electronic, mechanical,
photocopying, recording or otherwise, without the prior
written permission of the publishers.

OST
Food
641.5636

a Vegetarian Christmas

Rose Elliot is Britain's foremost vegetarian cookery writer and her books have won her popular acclaim in all parts of the English-speaking world.

Rose has been in the vanguard of the revolution in our eating habits in recent years, as more and more people consume less meat and take greater interest in healthy eating. She frequently contributes to magazines, gives cookery demonstrations and broadcasts on radio and television. Rose is also a professional astrologer and, with her husband, runs a computer-based astrological service which provides personality profiles, forecasts and compatibility charts. (For more details, please send SAE to Rose Elliot, PO Box 16, Eastleigh SO5 6BH, UK.)

C0000 002 227 000

Other Thorsons books by Rose Elliot

the Bean Book
Vegan Feasts
Cheap and Easy
Low Fat, Low Sugar

OSTERLEY LIBRARY

C2 22 7 000   7/05

contents

celebrating christmas

I love Christmas. The fun, the memories, the spicy smells, the goodwill. Yes, like everyone else I deplore the exploitation and the pressures, the Christmas catalogues dropping through the letter box before the end of the summer and the carols being played in shops in November, but however much I may grumble about these things, the Christmas magic always gets to me in the end.

We always had especially wonderful Christmases when I was a child. My parents, sister and I, along with my aunt, uncle and cousins, always spent Christmas with my grandparents in their house in the country. This was great fun, with lots of excitement and racing around the house and garden, as well as singing – and listening to – carols, a beautiful service on Christmas Eve in the chapel there, and a short meditation at noon on Christmas Day. Then we had Christmas dinner, and opened all the presents which were kept under the tree until after the Queen's speech.

What really made Christmas special, though, was my grandmother's approach to it. My grandmother, Grace Cooke, was a very remarkable woman, a mystic and seer. Although she considered herself to be a Christian, and had a deep love and respect for Jesus, she thought of Christmas as being symbolic of an older, universal truth, not confined to the Christian church. She saw the birth of the baby Jesus in a dark cave or in a stable, as a symbol of the awakening of the light of love in every human heart.

It was her belief (and mine, too) that all of us have that light of love – the spark of divinity – within ourselves. We express it when we give and receive love, and it is at these times we feel happy within ourselves; but when we cut ourselves off from that centre, we become out of sorts with ourselves and others. We are probably most aware of this power when we fall in love – our heart really opens, and everything seems magical. We also notice it at Christmas, when we think about other people more than we usually do and there is a general feeling of goodwill and the dropping of barriers.

The sense of universality and brotherhood which this approach to Christmas gives appeals to me very much: no race or religious creed is excluded; the awakening of the light of love in our hearts is something which we can all experience and celebrate. For me it is especially significant that Christmas is at the time of the winter solstice when, in the northern hemisphere the sun – or light – begins to get closer to us again.

All are reasons for celebration, of which preparing and eating wonderful meals together is a natural and important part. Christmas cooking is, for most people, the great culinary feast, not to say feat, of the year. Even people who do not do a great deal of cooking during the rest of the year find themselves doing so at Christmas and need good, reliable recipes. This is especially true if they find themselves having to cook for one or more of the increasing number of vegetarians!

This chapter aims to answer this need. It's a collection of all the tips, ideas and best recipes for Christmas that I've gathered over the years, as well as exciting new ones. So whether you've just one vegetarian to cater for, or a crowd, or just want some fresh and delicious ideas for festive food, I hope you'll find it helpful: an inspiring and practical cook's companion.

One of the great pleasures of traditional Christmas cooking is that not only can it be done well in advance, but it's actually all the better for it. So when new supplies of plump dried fruit fill the shops, you can fill the house with the warm and spicy smells of Christmas and get the cake, pudding and mincemeat made and stored away, knowing that they will only improve with time. Shopping for ingredients and equipment, and the making of these delicious, traditional dishes, can be fitted in over several days and weeks, giving you a chance to produce them when it is convenient for you.

Good Christmas planning can begin as early as October, with the listing and buying of ingredients, the checking of equipment, the making of menu plans and the gradual filling up of the store-cupboard and freezer. Done in this relaxed and gradual way, Christmas preparations can be enjoyed as the pleasure they really are. One of the bonuses is that there is time for other people, especially the children, to join in if they wish, which adds to the fun and sense of anticipation. Then, when Christmas arrives, with the majority of the work done, you can relax with everyone else, and have a really good time. I have found that the earlier I make my preparations, the more I enjoy them – and the more I enjoy Christmas itself.

Even the best-laid Christmas plans don't always work out the way you would like them to, and there have been times when I have been making a Christmas cake in the week before Christmas and icing it on Christmas Eve. So in this book you'll find a wonderful Last Minute Christmas Cake, as well as plenty of not-too-demanding but rather special recipes for every meal, since I know that even people who don't cook or entertain a great deal during the year find that they do so at Christmas, either through desire or necessity. I hope you'll enjoy them.

I've also considered the fact that many people are, I know, cooking for one or more vegetarians as well as for meat-eaters. Under these circumstances, there are two courses of action: sometimes everyone can enjoy a completely vegetarian meal; at other times, you can share the vegetables and accompaniments (as long as these are made without animal products like meat stock, gelatine or dripping etc), and the vegetarians can have their own main course.

Often, in practice, I've found that the meat-eaters like to share this, too, as a kind of extra side-dish to their meat, so you need to make enough. I rather like it when this happens; I certainly like to avoid a 'them' and 'us' approach, more a mutual acceptance of dietary preferences and a sharing of food. Of course, this does inevitably mean extra work for the cook, which is where advance preparation is such a help.

Most of the main courses in this chapter freeze really well, as do parts of the meal, such as crêpes, sauces, stuffings, pastry cases and so on, so that if you have some of these stashed away in the freezer, you can combine them with fresh vegetables, eggs, milk or cheese (if they eat these) and put together a delicious dish for one or two unexpected vegetarians in no time at all.

You'll find my specific freezer recommendations and standby recipes later in this section. But to begin the preparations, and get yourself in the mood early, I recommend that you stick with tradition and make the cake, the pudding and the pies first.

traditional christmas cake

Put the dried fruit into a bowl with the candied peel. Rinse and halve the cherries and add to the bowl, along with the sherry or orange juice. Mix, then cover and leave for 1–2 days, stirring once or twice each day.

Set the oven to 140°C/275°F/Gas 1. Line a 20 cm/8 inch round cake tin (pan) with a double layer of greaseproof (waxed) paper, and tie a double layer of newspaper around the outside.

Sift together the flours, baking powder and spices. Cream the butter with the sugar until light and fluffy, then beat the eggs in a little at a time, adding some of the flour mixture if there is any sign of curdling. Fold in the flour mixture, then stir in the dried fruit, orange and lemon rind and both types of almonds. Spoon the mixture into the cake pan and bake for 4–4½ hours, until a skewer inserted into the middle of the cake comes out clean. Stand the cake in its pan on a wire rack to cool.

Remove the cake from the tin (pan), strip off the paper, prick the cake all over with a skewer, and pour the brandy over it. Wrap in greaseproof paper and store in an airtight tin until needed. It will keep well for 1–3 months and 'mature' during that time. Sprinkle a little more brandy over the top occasionally if you like during storage.

makes one 20 cm/ 8 inch round cake

750 g/1½ lb/4½ cups mixed dried fruit
100 g/4 oz/¾ cup candied peel, chopped
225 g/8 oz/1½ cups glacé (candied) cherries
150 ml/5 fl oz/⅔ cup sherry or orange juice
250 g/9 oz plain wholewheat flour or a half-and-half mix of plain white (all-purpose) flour and wholewheat flour
1 tsp baking powder
½ tsp ground mixed spice
¼ tsp freshly grated nutmeg
250 g/9 oz/1 cup butter
250 g/9 oz/scant 1½ cups soft brown sugar
4 eggs, lightly beaten
grated rind of 1 orange
grated rind of 1 lemon
50 g/2 oz/⅔ cup ground almonds
50 g/2 oz/⅔ cup flaked almonds
2 tbsp brandy

almond paste

makes about 700 g/ 1¹⁄₂ lb, enough for a 20 cm/8 inch round cake

200 g/7 oz/2¹⁄₃ cups ground almonds

200 g/7 oz/1 cup caster sugar

200 g/7 oz/scant 1¹⁄₂ cups icing sugar

1 tbsp lemon juice

2 eggs, beaten

a few drops of almond extract

Put the almonds into a large bowl with the caster (superfine) sugar, then sift in the icing (confectioners') sugar. Add the lemon juice, then gradually mix in the beaten eggs, adding enough to make a stiff paste. Don't knead the mixture too much or it may get oily.

TO PUT THE PASTE ON THE CAKE

First prepare the cake by coating it with jam (jelly) to make the almond paste stick. If you are using apricot jam, sieve 2 tablespoonfuls into a small saucepan, or use redcurrant or other jelly, which avoids the need for sieving. Add a tablespoonful of water and heat gently until melted.

Use two-thirds of the almond paste to roll out a strip the height of the cake and the same length as the cake's circumference. Gather up the trimmings, and roll these, and the remaining almond paste, to make a circle just slightly larger than the top of the cake. You might prefer to use the cake upside down, as the base is usually flatter than the top. Brush this with some of the melted jam or jelly – don't do the sides yet. Holding the cake by the sides, put it, jammy-side down, on to the circle of almond paste. Now turn it up the right way, brush the sides with jam and, holding the top and bottom of the cake between your flat hands, place the side of the cake on the strip of almond paste and simply roll it along – the almond paste will stick to it.

Gently press together the join where the ends meet, then put the cake on a board and leave to dry for 24 hours before serving or covering with icing.

royal icing

Beat the egg whites and glycerine together, then add the sugar, a little at a time, beating well after each addition. After adding half the sugar, add the lemon juice. Continue adding the remaining sugar, beating to incorporate, until the mixture forms stiff peaks.

VEGAN VERSION
For vegan icing, use a thick glacé icing (page 170).

TO ROYAL ICE THE CAKE
Spoon the icing on to the cake, on top of the almond paste. Use a spatula to draw the icing thickly and evenly all over the top and sides, then use it to flick up decorative peaks.

TO DECORATE
Swirl about 12 thin red ribbons around a candle centrepiece, curling them so that they fall prettily over the cake. As a finishing touch, arrange some holly sprigs and berries on the top.

makes enough for a 20 cm/8 inch round cake

2 egg whites
2 tsp glycerine
700 g/1$\frac{1}{2}$ lb icing (confectioners') sugar, sifted, plus extra for dusting
juice of $\frac{1}{2}$ small lemon

fondant icing

makes enough to ice and decorate a 20 cm/8 inch round cake

450 g/1 lb icing (confectioners') sugar, sifted, plus extra for dusting

50 g/2 oz/¼ cup liquid glucose

1 egg white

Mix all the ingredients together to make a stiff, mouldable paste. If you wish, you can use store-bought fondant icing, in which case, you will need 90 g/2 lb to cover the cake.

TO FONDANT ICE THE CAKE

Roll the icing out, using sifted icing (confectioners') sugar to dust if necessary, to make a piece large enough to cover the top and sides of the cake. Lift this up carefully by putting your flat hands underneath it, then gently lower it over the cake, letting it fall down the sides. Ease the icing round the sides of the cake and press it gently into position. Trim all the extra icing away. Leave for 6–8 hours.

Meanwhile, gather up all the trimmings which you can colour if you like, re-roll and cut into interesting shapes with pastry cutters to decorate the top and sides of the cake.

TO DECORATE

Cut out holly leaf shapes and arrange them around the top outside edge of the cake and around the base, on a silver cake board. To add to the festive feeling, put some small silver cake-decorating balls on top of each holly leaf and some real holly leaves in a circle in the middle, surrounding a Christmas candle. As a special finishing touch, arrange some Christmas jasmine flowers next to the holly leaves. To make them, use a fine brush to paint fresh jasmine flowers with a lightly whisked egg white (just enough to break it up – add a drop or two of water if it's too viscous). Then lightly sprinkle with caster (superfine) sugar and leave to dry at room temperature or in a very cool oven. Just before serving, tie a ribbon round the cake to complete the decoration.

OTHER IDEAS FOR FONDANT ICING

Decorate the sides and top of the cake with interesting fondant shapes – and paint them with cake colourings. Angels round the sides with one on top would be appropriately festive; or you could stamp out lots of Christmas stars and scatter them over the top and sides of the cake.

A favourite fondant idea of mine is to ice the cake, then cut out some green fondant leaves – use green cake colouring to get the right colour – to go in the middle. Put a red candle in the middle of the 'leaves' and, around it, Christmas roses, also made from fondant icing. It's quite easy to mould them – stick five white 'petals' round a gold 'stamen' with egg white; about five 'roses' should fit nicely around the candle. Finish with a red ribbon around the side.

OTHER CAKE DECORATIONS

You could use almond paste on its own. Flute it attractively around the top of the cake as you would flute a pie, then perhaps lightly score in a criss-cross pattern with a knife. Arrange a candle and holly, or marzipan fruit, in the middle and tie a toning ribbon round the outside.

Or try a jewel-bright topping of crystallized fruits and brazil nuts, halved pecans and whole cashew nuts or blanched almonds. Stick these on to the top of the cake in an attractive pattern with warmed clear honey, and brush over with more warmed honey to glaze. For a sparkling finish, brush over the whole cake with clear honey, then sprinkle with preserving sugar or even some coloured coffee sugar and little silver balls.

vegetarian christmas pudding

serves 6

125 g/4 oz/³/₄ cup + 2 tbsp
plain wholewheat flour or a
half-and-half mix of plain
white (all-purpose) flour
and wholewheat flour
1 tsp baking powder
125 g/4 oz/¹/₂ cup pure
vegetable fat
125 g/4 oz/scant ³/₄ cup
dark brown sugar
450 g/1 lb/3 cups mixed
dried fruit
125 g/4 oz/³/₄ cup candied
peel, chopped
125 g/4 oz/2 cups soft
breadcrumbs
25 g/1 oz/¹/₃ cup flaked
almonds
grated rind of 1 orange
grated rind of 1 lemon
¹/₂ tsp ground ginger
¹/₂ tsp grated nutmeg
1¹/₂ tsp ground mixed spice
1 tbsp black treacle
4 tbsp whisky
150 ml/5 fl oz/²/₃ cup stout

Sift the flour and baking powder on to a plate and leave on one side. Put the fat and sugar into a large bowl and beat until creamy, then add all the remaining ingredients, including the flour, and mix very well, to a thick, creamy consistency. Don't forget to wish! Cover the bowl and leave overnight.

Next day, put the mixture into a lightly greased 1.2 litre (2 pint) bowl (or two 600 ml/1 pint basins), cover with a circle of greased greaseproof (waxed) paper and put on a lid if there is one. If not, secure with some foil or a pudding cloth over the top. Steam for 6–8 hours. The longer a pudding is steamed, the darker and more richly flavoured it will become. Cool, then put a clean piece of greaseproof and a new foil or a fresh pudding cloth on top of the bowl and store the pudding in a cool, dry place until required.

Steam for a further 3 hours before eating.

TO FLAME A CHRISTMAS PUDDING

The important thing is to warm the brandy first. Put 4 tablespoons of brandy – or 2 tablespoons brandy and 2 tablespoons vodka, which is higher in alcohol so burns well – into a metal soup ladle and warm by holding over a gas flame or electric ring. Then quickly light the brandy and pour carefully over and round the pudding.

mincemeat

This deliciously moist and spicy mincemeat is fat free.

Mix everything together in a large bowl and set aside for 1–2 hours to allow the flavours to mingle. Transfer to a casserole, cover and bake at 180°C/350°F/Gas 4 for 1 hour. Cool, then store in an airtight jar until ready to use.

makes 1 kg/2¹/₂ lb

225 g/8 oz/1¹/₃ cups dried
pears, chopped
grated rind of 1 lemon
grated rind of 1 orange
450 g/1 lb/3 cups mixed
dried fruit
100 g/4 oz/³/₄ cup whole
candied peel, chopped
100 g/4 oz/³/₄ cup glacé
(candied) cherries, halved
100 g/4 oz/³/₄ cup dates,
chopped
50 g/2 oz/²/₃ cup flaked
almonds
1 tsp ground mixed spice
¹/₂ tsp grated nutmeg
¹/₂ tsp ground ginger
125 ml/4 fl oz/¹/₂ cup
medium sherry
90 ml/3 fl oz/¹/₃ cup brandy
90 ml/3 fl oz/¹/₃ cup water

mince pies

makes 12

**1 quantity rich pastry –
page 29**
**450 g/1 lb mincemeat –
previous page**
caster (superfine) sugar

Set the oven to 200°C/400°F/Gas 6 and lightly grease a shallow 12-hole bun tin (cup cake or muffin pan). On a lightly floured board, roll out the pastry thinly, then cut out twelve 7.5 cm/3 inch circles and twelve 6 cm/2½ inch circles using a round cutter. Press one of the larger circles gently into each section of the bun tin (pan), then put a teaspoonful of mincemeat on top and cover with the smaller pastry circles. Don't fill them too full, or they may ooze and burst as they cook. Press down at the edges, make a steamhole in the top, then bake for about 20 minutes, or until the pastry is lightly browned. Cool in the tin (pan).

Freeze until required. Serve warm, sprinkled with sugar.

making the
most of your freezer

I find it a help to make, about six weeks in advance if I'm organized, a rough menu plan for the main meals to be cooked over the Christmas period, so that I can freeze some of the dishes in advance. If you make your menu plan and list of dishes for the freezer in good time, it's easier and more enjoyable to fit in the extra cooking over the 4–6 weeks leading up to Christmas. You'll find ideas for menus for different types of meals in The Twelve Days of Christmas on page 14, as well as notes of the individual dishes that freeze well in other parts of the book. Some of the most useful standbys for the freezer are listed here.

DIPS AND FIRST COURSES

These are the last thing you want to be bothered with when you're busy, so having some of these frozen is a real help. Dips such as *hummus* and *baba ghanoush* freeze well; others, like soured cream and avocado, don't, but can be whizzed up in moments. Most soups freeze beautifully, and it's particularly handy to have a supply of special garnishes, such as crisp *sesame stars* or *croûtons*. Home-made *vegetable stock* is another good standby. Although there are some quite good stock cubes and powders on the market, nothing can compare with the delicacy of home-made stock, and if I haven't got any I tend to use water. One way of getting good stock without any bother is to save the water in which vegetables have been cooked. I keep this, covered, in a jug in the fridge or freeze some if there's extra.

SAUCES

Sauces are a most useful freezer item, often enabling you to create a meal from a few ingredients you happen to have in, or providing the finishing touch to a meal without much effort. I find you can never have too much *fresh tomato sauce* or *Italian tomato sauce* in the freezer. Thaw, heat and serve with pasta and you have a filling meal in minutes; spread on top of any number of different bases, such as French bread, baps, rolls or pitta breads, top with slices of tomato, sweet pepper, mushroom, or whatever you fancy, and grated cheese and a few black olives for quick pizzas; pour over lightly cooked vegetables, such as fennel, top with Parmesan cheese and serve as a light main course; or serve with a vegetarian burger, croquette or savoury loaf to add lots of colour and moisture to the meal.

Traditional Christmas Sauces – *bread sauce, cranberry sauce* and *gravy* – all freeze perfectly, and if you're planning to serve these, it's a great help to get them done in advance. The same applies to sweet sauces and accompaniments such as *brandy butter, rum sauce, vegan cream* and *Apricot* and *Raspberry coulis.*

VEGETABLES AND HERBS

On the whole, I prefer to use fresh vegetables for accompaniments, although there are some exceptions. It's always useful to have some *red and green peppers* in the freezer, either for a salad or to incorporate into another dish. *Festive red cabbage* also freezes well and is a useful dish for the freezer because it's good with many savoury dishes. Make it into a light main meal with the addition of roast, baked or mashed potatoes, and perhaps some cooked chestnuts. Dishes that can be cooked straight from frozen are particularly useful so I always try to keep some of these in the freezer – *light gratin dauphinois* and *parsley potato stars* are two favourites in this category. In addition to all of these, I like to keep a stock of plain vegetables such as petits pois, sweetcorn, green beans, broad (fava) beans, leaf spinach and, sorry to admit this, oven chips. Chopped fresh parsley is another good standby – in fact, most herbs freeze well and could be stored away for times when you haven't got any fresh.

BREAD AND PASTRY

Home-made rolls keep well in the freezer, as of course does any commercial bread. I like to keep a supply of our normal favourite wholewheat loaf, plus specials like baguettes, croissants, pitta bread, and perhaps some Italian ciabatta bread. White and wholewheat breadcrumbs, stored in plastic bags which can be topped up whenever you have bread over, are always useful to have, but especially so when you're making Christmas recipes. And if you like *garlic bread* it's a great help to have some prepared and wrapped in foil ready for baking. Don't do it too far in advance – no more than 1–2 weeks – the flavour of garlic can mysteriously decrease in the freezer.

A packet of filo and/or bought puff pastry is handy to have, too, and I like to store quiche or tart cases either uncooked or, more convenient, baked blind, for finishing with a quickly made filling. Many of the savoury pastry dishes in this book can also be frozen – see below and on the recipe pages for specific suggestions.

MAIN-COURSE DISHES

What main-course dishes you put in your freezer depends very much on your own taste and your menu plans. I find it useful to have some kind of frozen burgers, such as *Kate's butterbean croquettes*, so that I can take them out individually for giving kids' suppers and snacks at odd times. They can be cooked quickly from frozen. Terrines, savoury bakes and loaves are also useful and can be frozen raw, cooked or partially cooked. They're best thawed before cooking.

Savoury pastry dishes such as *flaky mushroom Christmas tree*, *chestnut and red wine pâté en croûte*, and *Christmas savoury strudel* freeze excellently; open-freeze them before baking, then wrap them well to protect any fragile garnishes. To use, loosen their wrappings and let them thaw completely, then bake as described in the recipe.

DESSERTS

Ice creams and sorbets are useful freezer basics, and can be quickly made more special if you serve them with your own frozen fruit coulis or supply of purées and some thin, crisp sweet biscuits (cookies) or tuiles; or a favourite with my children as well as with adults, *meringue nests*. Ready-made meringues are a particularly useful extra to have available at Christmas. Other made-up desserts will depend on your menus, but *chocolate charlotte* as well as traditional *bûche de noël* freeze well, as do most cheesecakes and old-fashioned trifles. I also find it useful to keep one or two sweet pastry dishes over and above mince pies as they are so popular with my family.

CAKES

I'm not keen on giving up freezer space to foods that store well in other ways, so I never keep rich fruit cakes or gingerbread in the freezer, although both are good for Christmas. Both can be made in advance and kept in a tin, as can lighter cakes such as *Madeira cake*, *vegan chocolate sponge cake*, *light ginger cake with lemon icing*, if they're made just before you want them; but if you want to get ahead with these they freeze very well and can be made and decorated before freezing – open-freeze them so that they are hard before you wrap them, and pack them carefully to avoid damage.

THE TWELVE DAYS OF CHRISTMAS...

Christmas Eve though not, strictly speaking, one of the traditional 'twelve days', is, for most of us, the start of Christmas, as friends and family gather for this very special, and I think rather magical, night of the year.

The planning of the meal on Christmas Eve will, of course, depend on circumstances: whether people are arriving late, from far away, perhaps; whether you're planning to go to Midnight Mass ... In some families, the food on this night is as traditional as Christmas Dinner. I feel that the ideal meal for Christmas Eve is something festive, but different enough from Christmas Dinner not to rival it. Also, since however well organized you are Christmas Eve always seems to be a busy time of last-minute shopping, present-wrapping and beginning the preparations for Christmas Day, it should either be fairly easy to make, or something which you can freeze in advance and just heat through.

A meal that I think meets all these criteria is *Christmas couscous*. This consists of several bowls of different mixtures: the grain (couscous), the lightly spiced, colourful vegetable stew, and as many extras – such as chick peas (garbanzo beans), raisins, chutneys and pickles, pine nuts – as you want to serve. You can pass the bowls around the table and everyone can help themselves, which gets things off to a friendly start and somehow adds to the feeling of celebration. This meal is easy to do but all the extras make it look as if you've taken a good deal more trouble than you have. A simple first course, such as *festive spring rolls*, or a dip like guacamole with some crisp fresh vegetables or warm pitta bread, goes well with this, as does a dessert such as *orange slices with flower water*. If people are going to church you might like to save the dessert for later and make it something warming and substantial to eat on their return, like hot *mince pies*, for instance, or *Swedish ring cake*. Or serve some good chunky bread or home-made biscuits (cookies) with a good selection of cheese and pickles, nuts and fruit.

One of the Christmas Dinner menus in this book would also be ideal for a special Christmas Eve meal – I've given quite a variety of suggestions in a later chapter, so it's quite possible to use one on Christmas Eve and another for Christmas Day itself. Round the meal off with a light and delicious dessert such as the ice cream *Christmas bombe*, *rum-macerated fruits with coconut and lime cream* or *lemon and ginger cheesecake*. Another meal I'm fond of is the *flaky mushroom Christmas tree* with its fresh and tangy creamy herb sauce; or, for a festive yet light meal, I also very much like *chestnut-stuffed*

mushrooms served with *festive red cabbage* and *potatoes with lemon*, or my own version of the French classic, creamy *light gratin dauphinois*.

It's a good idea to decide on your Christmas Dinner menu – one of the most important meals of the year – first, before you plan any of the others, and choose your other meals accordingly. There are lots of ideas for this in the Christmas Dinner chapter, and each menu comes complete with countdown timetables to make sure that everything goes really smoothly, and that you enjoy the meal as much as everyone else. Whether you have Christmas Dinner at lunchtime or in the evening, you will probably want something light for the other meal of the day. My family is incurably traditional; having known only vegetarian Christmases, they always want the most traditional of vegetarian meals on Christmas Day: *cashew nut roast* served with roast potatoes, gravy, cranberry sauce and all the other trimmings. I make enough of the roast lunch to have it sliced cold in the evening with salad and pickles, followed by trifle, ice cream or hot mince pies.

Other ideas for a light yet Christmassy second meal of the day would be *festive spring rolls*, which can be frozen or *tagliatelle with creamy walnut sauce*, both of which I'd serve with a simple salad – mixed leaf, shredded lettuce or lettuce heart, for instance. If you're feeling really full, several dips of different colours, with some fresh vegetables such as radishes, spring (green) onions and slices of lettuce heart, plus some bread, biscuits, crackers, crisps (chips) or tortilla chips, can be surprisingly successful and great fun to eat.

On the days following Christmas, fresh, light food seems to be what people fancy most – and it must either be quick and easy to make or eminently freezable. Some of our favourites are *clear watercress soup; lemony vegetables* served with light and creamy mashed potatoes or mixed rice; my daughter *Kate's butterbean croquettes* or *little brie and hazelnut bakes*, both of which are delicious with some fruity home-made *cranberry sauce* and *avocado with curried Brazil nut stuffing*. Desserts that are particularly good at this time are *lemon and ginger cheesecake* and the refreshing *Christmas dried fruit salad*.

christmas

october

- Find recipes for Christmas Cake, Vegetarian Christmas Pudding and Mincemeat.

- Make lists of ingredients needed and start buying items such as dried fruit, which store well.

- Check equipment: now is the time to buy new tins and pans – the stronger and heavier the better – pudding bowls, pastry cutters or anything special needed in Christmas recipes.

- Save jars for the mincemeat and any other Christmas preserves.

- Check supplies of foil (the narrow type is most convenient), nonstick and greaseproof (waxed) paper, plastic bags, clingfilm and labels for the freezer.

- If you're expecting to have a large party at Christmas and have limited freezer space, collect polystyrene boxes (styrofoam) and packing, and get some freezer ice packs – these are good for keeping food cold for short periods of time when the fridge and freezer are full.

- Clear out the freezer and start using any items which need eating up to give you plenty of freezer space for Christmas.

october/november

- Make the Christmas Cake, Vegetarian Christmas Pudding and Mincemeat. Keep them in a cool, dry place.

timetable

november

- Think about Christmas menus and any special dishes you want to try; check that you have the equipment needed.

- Make a plan of dishes to prepare for the freezer, and a rough timetable; most dishes keep well in the freezer for 4–6 weeks.

- From mid-November onwards, you can start freezing dishes for Christmas.

december

- The more you can get into the freezer during the first fortnight the better.

- Make and freeze Mince Pies, Brandy Butter and Rum Sauce.

- Finalise Christmas Dinner menu. Make and freeze main courses and sauces as applicable. Some first courses, such as Iced Melon Soup with Violets can be frozen, too.

- During the second week, put almond paste and icing on your Christmas cake.

vegetable stock

makes about 1–1.25 litres/ 1³/₄–2¹/₄ pints/ 5–6 cups

900 g/2 lb mixed vegetables, for instance, 2 onions, 3 celery stalks, 2 carrots, 1 turnip, 2 broccoli stalks
25 g/1 oz/2 tbsp butter or white vegetable fat
1.5 litres/2¹/₂ pints/6¹/₄ cups water
5 cloves garlic – no need to peel, just halve
12 peppercorns
2 bayleaves
a bunch of parsley, or just the stems
a few sprigs of fresh thyme, or
1 tsp dried

Scrub and roughly chop the vegetables. Melt the butter or fat in a large saucepan, add the vegetables and fry, for 10 minutes until soft. Add the water, garlic, peppercorns, bayleaves, parsley and thyme. Bring to the boil, cover and simmer very gently for about 40 minutes, until the vegetables are very soft. Leave the pot to stand until it's completely cold, then skim the fat from the surface. This stock keeps for a few days in the fridge and also freezes well: old cream or yogurt cartons make good containers.

fresh tomato sauce

Even in winter when tomatoes don't have that warm, sun-drenched flavour, I prefer this sauce to the more strongly flavoured kind made from canned tomatoes, although both are useful. This one is good for serving with delicately flavoured foods, and my children love it with pasta of any shape. It's also good with boiled rice tossed with a few fresh herbs. In fact, I find I can't make too much of it. You can vary the basic sauce by adding chopped fresh herbs such as basil and oregano, sliced button mushrooms, crushed garlic or a dash of red wine.

In a large saucepan, fry the onion in the oil for 10 minutes, until soft but not browned. Add the tomatoes and cook for about 10 minutes, until they are soft but still bright in colour and fresh in flavour. Season with salt and pepper and freeze until required.

Usually I serve this sauce just as it is, which is fine for pasta and simple dishes, although it can be puréed in a food processor and then strained quickly through a sieve (strainer) if you want a smooth sauce. Ideally it would be useful to keep both types, the chunky and the smooth, in the freezer.

serves 6

1 onion, peeled and finely chopped
1 tbsp olive oil
1 kg/2 lb tomatoes, peeled and roughly chopped
sea salt
freshly ground black pepper

italian tomato sauce

This sauce has a stronger flavour than the Fresh Tomato Sauce on the previous page, and some people may prefer it. I find it particularly useful as a topping for home-made pizzas. Spoon it on top of any bases which happen to be handy; homemade bread ones if there's time, otherwise split and toasted rolls or muffins, round pitta bread, or slices of bread which have been dried out in a cool oven, like the bases of Italian crostini.

serves 6

1 onion, peeled and chopped

2 tbsp olive oil

2 cloves garlic, peeled and crushed

2 x 400 g/14 oz cans tomatoes

$^1/_2$ tsp dried basil

$^1/_2$ tsp dried oregano

1 bayleaf

150 ml/5 fl oz/$^2/_3$ cup red wine, stock or water

sea salt

freshly ground black pepper

In a large saucepan, fry the onion in the oil for 10 minutes, until soft but not browned. Add the garlic, tomatoes and juice, basil, oregano, bayleaf and the wine, stock or water. Cook gently for 20 minutes, until the tomatoes have almost reduced to a purée. Remove the bay leaf, then purée the sauce in a blender or food processor. Season with salt and pepper. A little extra liquid can be added at this point for a thinner sauce. Freeze until required.

cranberry sauce

You may wish to make more sauce than the quantity given here, for serving with several meals over Christmas. Freeze in suitable sized containers and reheat gently before serving.

Put the cranberries into a saucepan with the water. Bring to the boil, then simmer until the berries are tender, about 4–5 minutes. Add the sugar and cook gently until dissolved.

Remove from the heat and add the port or orange juice, if you're using these. Either serve warm or freeze until required.

serves 6

125 g/4 oz/1 cup cranberries, washed and picked over

4 tbsp water

50 g/2 oz/¹/₃ cup sugar

1 tbsp port or orange juice – optional

bread sauce

serves 6

3 cloves

1 onion, peeled

300 ml/10 fl oz/1¼ cups
milk

1 bayleaf

50 g/2 oz white bread,
crusts removed

15 g/½ oz/1 tbsp butter

2 tbsp cream

sea salt

freshly ground black pepper

grated nutmeg

Stick the cloves into the onion, then put the onion into a saucepan with the milk and bayleaf. Bring to the boil then take off the heat, add the bread, cover and leave on one side for 15–30 minutes to allow the flavours to infuse.

Remove the onion and the bayleaf. Beat the mixture to break up the bread, and stir in the butter, cream, salt, pepper and grated nutmeg to taste. Either serve warm or freeze until required.

VEGAN VERSION

Use vegan margarine instead of butter, soya milk instead of milk and omit the cream.

béchamel sauce

This sauce will keep, well covered, in the fridge, for at least a few days.

Melt the butter in a large saucepan. Add the flour, stir over the heat for a couple of minutes, then add the milk, a quarter at a time, mixing well between each addition. Add the onion, celery, carrot, bayleaf, peppercorns, thyme and mace and leave to simmer gently for 10–15 minutes. Strain the sauce through a sieve (strainer) into a clean saucepan. Season with salt, pepper and grated nutmeg, and use as appropriate, with vegetables, pasta or other savouries.

VEGAN VERSION
Use vegan margarine instead of butter and soya milk instead of dairy milk.

PARSLEY SAUCE
Add 2–4 tbsp chopped fresh parsley and a few drops of lemon juice to taste to the sauce after straining.

**makes 450 ml/
³/₄ pint/2 cups**

25 g/1 oz/2 tbsp butter
25 g/1 oz/3 tbsp plain
(all-purpose) flour
600 ml/1 pint/2¹/₂ cups
milk
piece of onion, celery and
scraped carrot
1 bayleaf
6 black peppercorns
a sprig of thyme
1–2 blades of mace
salt
freshly ground black pepper
grated nutmeg

garlic bread

I love crisp, hot, buttery garlic bread and could eat it with almost any soup or salad. Assuming that others share my passion, I find it very useful to have some loaves already spread with butter, wrapped in foil and stored in the freezer, ready to pop straight into the oven. I've given quantities for one normal-size French stick here, but I generally make up more while I'm about it. It's sometimes convenient to freeze the bread in smaller amounts, perhaps a quarter of a loaf firmly wrapped in foil. As the garlic flavour lessens during freezing, it's best not to keep it for more than 3–4 weeks, and 1–2 weeks is better.

1 French stick (baguette)
75 g/3 oz/6 tbsp soft butter
2–4 fat cloves garlic, peeled and crushed

Cut the bread into 2.5 cm/1 inch diagonal slices without cutting right through to the base. Mash the butter with the garlic until it's thoroughly blended, then spread both sides of each slice of bread with the butter mixture. Press the loaf together and wrap in foil – or make two packages if this is more convenient and will fit your oven better. To use immediately, bake at 200°C/400°F/Gas 6 for 20 minutes, or until it's hot inside and crisp on the outside; or freeze until required, then bake from frozen for 30 minutes.

vegan cream

In a small bowl, blend the cornflour (cornstarch) to a paste with a little of the soya milk. Put the rest of the milk into a saucepan with the vanilla pod (bean) and bring to the boil, pour over the cornflour (cornstarch) mixture, stir, and return to the pan. Stir until the mixture thickens, then remove from the heat and leave until completely cold.

In another bowl, beat the margarine until it's light and creamy, then gradually whisk in the cooled cornflour (cornstarch) mixture, avoiding the vanilla pod (bean), which can be rinsed, dried and used again. It's important to add the cornflour (cornstarch) mixture gradually, whisking well, to produce a beautiful light whipped cream. Add the sugar towards the end, a teaspoonful at a time, tasting the mixture to get it just right.

The delicate vanilla flavour can be enhanced with a drop or two of vanilla extract, or you can add a dash of brandy or rum, or orange or rose flour water, depending on what you're serving it with.

serves 4–6

3 tsp cornflour (cornstarch)
150 ml/5 fl oz/²/₃ cup
unsweetened soya milk
1 vanilla pod (bean)
90 g/3¹/₂ oz/7 tbsp soft
pure vegetable margarine
2–3 tsp icing
(confectioners') sugar
a few drops of vanilla
extract – optional

meringue nests

makes 6

2 egg whites
pinch of cream of tartar
125 g/4 oz/heaping ¹/₂ cup
caster (superfine) sugar

Set the oven to 150°C/300°F/Gas 2 and draw six 7.5 cm/3 inch circles well apart on greaseproof (waxed) or non-stick paper. Place the paper on a baking sheet, grease with butter or oil and sprinkle with flour.

Put the egg whites into a clean, grease-free bowl with the cream of tartar and whisk until stiff and dry. You should be able to turn the bowl upside down without the egg whites falling out. Whisk in half the sugar, then add the remaining sugar and whisk well.

Put the mixture into a piping bag fitted with a large shell nozzle (tip) and pipe circles round and round within the circles on the paper, then a final circle on top of the outermost circle, to form a nest shape.

Put the meringues into the oven, then reduce the setting to 110°C/200°F/Gas ¹/₄ and bake for 1¹/₂–2 hours, or until they are dried out. Turn the oven off and leave them to cool in the oven. Remove the meringues from the baking sheet with a palette knife (metal spatula). Either cool and use immediately or arrange carefully in a lidded container, cover and freeze until required.

apricot coulis

Put the apricots into a saucepan, cover with plenty of water and leave to soak overnight.

Next day, add the sugar and more water if necessary, so that the apricots are well covered. Bring to the boil, then let them simmer, uncovered, for about an hour, or until nearly all the water has gone and the apricots are very tender and bathed in a glossy syrup. Leave to cool.

Whizz the apricots and syrup thoroughly in a blender or food processor, adding some water to make a smooth purée. If necessary, add more water to thin the purée to a pouring consistency – like double (heavy) cream, or even a bit thinner. Pour into suitable containers for freezing – old cream or yogurt cartons with a snap-on plastic lid are ideal – label and freeze. To use, thaw, then gently heat if you want to serve it hot.

serves 6

225 g/8 oz/heaping 1 cup dried apricots
25 g/1 oz/2 tbsp caster (superfine) sugar

raspberry coulis

Whizz the raspberries with the water and sugar in a blender or food processor, then sieve (strain) the mixture into a saucepan. Bring to the boil and boil for 1 minute, to make the sauce clear and glossy. Cool, then either serve warm or freeze as required.

serves 6

450 g/1 lb raspberries – frozen are fine
2 tbsp water
2 tbsp caster (superfine) sugar

rum sauce

If you make this sauce in advance, cover with dots of butter to prevent a skin from forming.

serves 6

25 g/1 oz/2 tbsp butter

25 g/1 oz/3 tbsp cornflour (cornstarch)

600 ml/1 pint/2¹/₂ cups milk

25 g/1 oz/2 tbsp caster (superfine) sugar

4–6 tbsp single (light) cream

2–3 tbsp rum

Melt the butter in a medium-sized saucepan. Add the cornflour (cornstarch) and stir for a few seconds before pouring in the milk, one third at a time, whisking well after each addition. Simmer for a couple of minutes, then stir in the sugar, cream and rum. Either use immediately or tip into a suitable container and freeze until required.

rich pastry

Sift the flour and salt into a bowl or food processor. Add the butter, cut into pieces, add the egg yolk and water, and either mix with a fork until combined or whizz for a few seconds without the plunger to let in more air, to make a medium-soft dough.

This pastry freezes excellently, both cooked and uncooked. To store, wrap loosely and freeze.

makes about 250 g/9 oz

140 g/5 oz/1 cup plain wholewheat flour or a half-and-half mix of plain white (all-purpose) flour and wholewheat flour
pinch of salt
90 g/3$\frac{1}{2}$ oz/7 tbsp butter
1 egg yolk
1 tbsp water

Although we tend to think in terms of Christmas cooking as being the Dinner, in fact for most of us it involves a great deal more, especially now that the Christmas holiday seems to last longer and longer, requiring, I've found, food which is special and festive, but which is also refreshing and a good contrast to Christmas Dinner and the traditional pudding, mince pies and cake ... So the recipes in this section are for all the other meals that Christmas cooking involves, apart from the big day itself and parties.

As far as I'm concerned, such meals must either be quick and easy to make or good for freezing, so that they need the minimum of time and effort to produce on the day. I hope you'll agree that the dishes which follow meet these criteria. There are recipes for light savouries and dips, which can be used as first courses or, with the addition of some salad and bread, become snack meals in themselves. The same applies to the soups, which make particularly warming, filling winter meals, yet are easy on preparation and washing up.

If there are young children in the party, it's helpful to have some dishes in the freezer which enable you to take out a small portion and heat it up when required, for giving the kids an early supper before they go to bed, or snacks at odd times to fit in with their routine.

festive spring rolls

First make the sauce, which can be done some time in advance and kept in the fridge. Quarter the red peppers and remove the seeds. Place the peppers in a saucepan with the garlic cloves, cover with water and boil for 10–15 minutes, until the peppers are tender. Drain, liquidize, then pour the mixture through a sieve (strainer). Season with salt and pepper.

To make the spring rolls, if you're going to bake them straight away, set the oven to 200°C/400°F/ Gas 6. In a frying pan, fry the onions and carrots in the oil for 7 minutes, until almost soft. Add the beansprouts and ginger and fry, for a further 2–3 minutes, until all the vegetables are cooked. Add the Soy sauce and season with salt and pepper. Cool.

Cut a sheet of filo pastry in half, or divide it so that you have a piece measuring about 18 cm/7 inches square. Place a good heap of the mixture about 1 cm/½ inch from the top and well clear of the sides, then fold over the top and the sides and roll up, to make a neat parcel. Place on a baking sheet which has been brushed with olive oil. Make the rest of the spring rolls in the same way and arrange on the baking sheet. Brush the spring rolls lightly with olive oil and bake for about 20 minutes, turning them over after about 10 minutes so that both sides get crisp.

Serve the rolls on individual plates on a pool of the red pepper sauce, garnished with spring (green) onions, pepper slices and carrot curls.

makes about 20

2 onions, peeled and chopped
2 carrots, scraped and diced
1 tbsp olive oil, plus extra for brushing
350 g/12 oz/1½ cups beansprouts
1 tsp grated fresh ginger
1 tbsp Soy sauce
350 g/12 oz filo pastry

for the sauce:
2 large sweet red peppers
2–4 cloves garlic, peeled
sea salt
freshly ground black pepper

to garnish:
spring (green) onion tassels
thin sweet pepper slices
carrot curls

winter vegetable soup

The rouille on top of this soup adds a delicious warming touch, but it can be left off if you want a simpler version. You could stir in some soured cream or Greek yogurt instead, or top each bowlful with grated cheese, for a warming and filling winter meal.

serves 4

1 large onion
2 leeks
225 g/8 oz celeriac (celery root) or outer stalks of celery
2 tbsp olive oil
400 g/14 oz can tomatoes
1.2 litres/2 pints/ water or vegetable stock
sea salt
freshly ground black pepper
chilli powder

rouille – opposite page
croûtons – opposite page

Peel and chop the onion. Clean, trim and slice the leeks, keeping as much of the green part as you can. Peel the celeriac (celery root) and cut into 1 cm/½ inch dice. If you are using celery, cut it into smaller dice as it takes a long time to soften.

Heat the oil in a large saucepan, then put in all the vegetables. Cook over a gentle heat, with a lid on the pan, for 10–15 minutes, stirring every so often and not allowing them to brown. Add the tomatoes with their liquid, then add the water or stock and bring to the boil. Simmer gently for 30–40 minutes, or until all the vegetables are tender. Season with salt and pepper.

Ladle the steaming hot soup into bowls and top each with a good spoonful of the rouille, some croûtons and a sprinkling of chilli powder – or let everyone help themselves to the extras.

rouille

This makes a rusty red rouille. For a vivid yellow rouille, use a golden yellow pepper instead of the red one.

Put the red pepper into a pan of water and bring to the boil. Simmer for about 10–15 minutes, or until the pepper is very tender. Meanwhile, if you are using a dried chilli, soak this in a little boiling water.

Drain the cooked red pepper and remove any stalk, then place in a food processor with the fresh or soaked dried chilli and whizz to a purée. Add the bread and whizz thoroughly, then gradually add the oil, whizzing all the time, or after each addition. It's a bit like making mayonnaise, but much easier and less risky. As you add the oil, the mixture will thicken to a lovely smooth cream. Season with salt and a pinch of chilli powder if you want it hotter. You can lighten the rouille mixture a bit by beating in a tablespoonful or two of boiling water if you wish.

1 small or 1/2 large sweet red pepper, deseeded
1 fresh or dried red chilli pepper, deseeded
50 g/2 oz white bread, broken into rough pieces
125 ml/4 fl oz/1/2 cup olive oil
sea salt
chilli powder

croûtons

These can be done well in advance – they keep excellently in the freezer too.

Set the oven to 150°C/300°F/Gas 2. Cut the crusts from the bread, then spread each side lightly with butter. Cut into small dice and place on a baking sheet.

Bake for 40–60 minutes, or until the croûtons are crisp and crunchy.

4 slices of wholewheat bread
25 g/1 oz/2 tbsp butter

carol singers' onion soup

Surely this soup – a vegetarian version of the classic French Onion Soup – must be the most warming of them all? Wonderful to come in to on a cold night, whether you've been singing for your supper or not!

serves 4–6

2 tbsp oil
900 g/2 lb onions, peeled and thinly sliced
4 tsp sugar
sea salt
freshly ground black pepper
1.75 litres/3 pints/3¾ pints stock
2 cloves garlic, peeled and crushed
soy sauce
lemon juice
4–6 slices of French stick (baguette)
125 g/4 oz/1 cup Gruyère or Cheddar cheese, grated

Heat the oil in a saucepan, add the onions and fry, for 10 minutes or until they are tender but not browned. Add the sugar and some salt and pepper, and continue to fry, for a further 15–20 minutes, until the onions become a deep golden brown. Don't let them burn. Add the stock and garlic, bring to the boil and let the soup simmer for about 10 minutes. Add soy sauce to taste, and a few drops of lemon juice, salt and pepper as necessary.

When you're ready to serve the soup, have some piping hot bowls ready. Put the bread on the grill (broiler) pan, top with the cheese, and grill (broil) for a few minutes, until the cheese has melted. Ladle the soup into the hot bowls, top each with a piece of cheesy bread, and serve at once.

clear watercress soup

This easy-to-make, refreshing soup is a good alternative to Celery and Stilton Soup in the Christmas Dinner on page 112, if you want something lighter, and vegan. Adding the watercress just before serving gives it a lovely bright colour and fresh flavour.

Wash, trim and finely shred the leeks, using as much of the green part as you can. Heat the oil in a large saucepan, add the leeks, and fry gently for about 10 minutes, or until they are tender. Add the water or stock, bring to the boil, then simmer for about 10 minutes. Chop the watercress, then add this to the soup, along with soy sauce to taste – probably 2–4 tablespoons. Season with a little salt and pepper if necessary. Reheat gently and serve.

serves 4–6

2 leeks

1 tbsp olive oil

1 litre/1³/₄ pints/1 quart water or stock

75 g/3 oz/3 cups watercress

soy sauce

sea salt

freshly ground pepper

pasta and broccoli béchamel

serves 2–3

225 g/8 oz broccoli

125 g/4 oz/¹/₃ cup short macaroni, shells or other pasta shapes

300 ml/10 fl oz/1¹/₄ cups Béchamel Sauce – page 23

sea salt

freshly ground black pepper

for the topping – optional:

fresh breadcrumbs

a little butter or grated cheese

Wash and trim the broccoli then divide it into smallish pieces. Cook it in 1 cm/¹/₂ inch of boiling water for 3–4 minutes, or until it is nearly tender. Drain and leave on one side.

Cook the pasta in a large panful of boiling water until that, too, is just tender – *al dente* – then drain it immediately.

Meanwhile, gently heat the béchamel sauce. Add the pasta and broccoli to the sauce, season, then stir gently over the heat until everything is really hot. Serve immediately, or pour the mixture into a shallow heatproof dish, top with fresh breadcrumbs and a little butter or grated cheese and put under the grill (broiler) until it's golden brown and crisp.

VEGAN VERSION

Use a béchamel sauce made with soya milk and vegan margarine, and use margarine for the topping, if you're adding this.

potatoes with lemon

The lemony tang is refreshing, and these potatoes are convenient to cook, because they can be prepared in advance, ready for baking, and don't need much attention once they're in the oven.

Set the oven to 190°C/375°F/ Gas 5. Choose even-sized potatoes and scrub them. Put them into a saucepan, cover with water and parboil them for 7 minutes or until they are almost tender. With a sharp knife, remove the skins and cut the potatoes in half lengthways. Melt the butter, then stir in the grated lemon rind. Brush this lemon butter all over the potatoes then put them in a single layer into a baking pan. Bake for about 45 minutes, or until they are golden and crisp, turning them over about half way through so they get evenly browned.

serves 6

700 g/1½ lb potatoes
40 g/1½ oz/3 tbsp butter
grated rind of 1 lemon
sea salt
freshly ground pepper

light gratin dauphinois

This lighter version of the delicious classic goes well with many of the savoury dishes in this book. I often serve it for a light meal with just a good crunchy mixed vegetable salad or some stir-fried vegetables – like Lemony Vegetables on page 42.

serves 4

900 g/2 lb potatoes
50 g/2 oz/4 tbsp butter, melted
1 clove garlic, peeled and crushed
1 onion, peeled and thinly sliced
sea salt
freshly ground black pepper
grated nutmeg
150 ml/5 fl oz/²/₃ cup single (light) cream

Set the oven to 180°C/350°F/Gas 4. Peel the potatoes and cut them into thin slices. Grease a shallow wide gratin dish with half the butter, then spread the crushed garlic around the base and sides. Layer the potatoes and onion in the casserole, seasoning them with salt, freshly ground black pepper and nutmeg as you go, then pour over the cream and remaining butter. Cover with foil. Bake for 1 hour, then remove the foil and bake for a further 30 minutes, or until golden brown.

parsley potato stars

These are popular with children; they freeze well and can be grilled (broiled) or baked from frozen.

Peel the potatoes and cut them into even-sized chunks, then boil in water to cover until they are tender. Drain really well, then dry a little over the heat. Mash with the butter, parsley and seasoning to taste, to make a smooth, very stiff consistency. Set the oven to 200°C/400°F/Gas 6.

Knead the mixture on a well-floured board, then press out to a depth of 1 cm/½ inch, and cut out star shapes. If you are using straight away, bake on a lightly oiled sheet for about 30 minutes until golden brown. If you are freezing them, bake for about 20 minutes until they are just set and beginning to brown, then cool and freeze.

serves 4–6

900 g/2 lb potatoes
25 g/1 oz/½ cup butter
25 g/1 oz/2 tbsp fresh
parsley, chopped
sea salt
freshly ground pepper
grated nutmeg
flour

santa's surprise parcels

The parcels are crêpes and the surprise is the choice of fillings inside them. This recipe makes 12 thin crêpes and the quantity of each filling mixture is enough for about 4 crêpes. The crêpes can be made well in advance and kept in the fridge or freezer until needed. The fillings can also be made ahead of time, so you can have a meal in minutes.

makes 12

125 g/4 oz/³/₄ cup + 2 tbsp
plain wholewheat flour or a
half-and-half mix of plain
white (all-purpose) flour
and wholewheat flour
a good pinch of sea salt
1 tbsp olive oil
2 medium eggs
300 ml/10 fl oz/1¹/₄ cups
milk and water, mixed
oil for frying
fillings of your choice –
opposite page

Make the crêpes. Put the flour into a food processor with the salt, oil, eggs and milk and water and whizz until blended.

Oil the base of a small frying pan with a pad of kitchen paper and 1 tsp olive oil, then heat it until a small drop of water flicked into it splatters immediately. Pour about 2 tablespoonfuls of the batter into the pan and immediately tip it so that the batter spreads all over the base. After a few seconds, when the bottom of the crêpe is lightly browned and the top set, flip it over using a palette knife (metal spatula) and your fingers, to cook the other side for a few seconds, then lift it out on to a plate.

Continue to cook more crêpes until all the mixture is used, piling them up on top of each other on the plate as they're done. You will probably need to regrease the frying pan after every 2–3 crêpes. Leave them to cool completely, then wrap the pile of crêpes in foil and keep in the fridge or freeze until required.

To finish, carefully arrange a good tablespoonful of the chosen filling in the middle of each crêpe and fold over the edges to make a parcel. Put this, seam side down, in a shallow gratin dish, packing them all in a single layer. They can be topped with 4–6 tbsp cream or sprinkled with some grated Parmesan. Bake in the oven preheated to 180°C/350°F/Gas 4 for 20 minutes, to heat them through.

fillings for crêpes

SPINACH AND RICOTTA
Cook 450 g/1 lb fresh spinach or 225 g/8 oz frozen leaf spinach. Drain well, really pressing out the liquid, then mix with 15 g/½ oz/1 tbsp butter, 50 g/2 oz/¼ cup ricotta cheese, salt, pepper and grated nutmeg.

SWEETCORN AND CREAM CHEESE
Thaw 125 g/4 oz/heaping ½ cup frozen sweetcorn kernels by putting them into a sieve (strainer) and pouring boiling water over them. Put them into a bowl with 125 g/4 oz/½ cup cream cheese or low-fat smooth white cheese. Mix well. Some chopped fresh chives can be added.

AVOCADO AND TABASCO
Peel, stone and dice 1 ripe avocado. Sprinkle with lemon juice, salt, pepper and Tabasco. A little crushed garlic, or some chopped fresh chives can be added.

CAMEMBERT AND PINE NUTS
Dice 225 g/8 oz Camembert cheese and mix with 50 g/2 oz/scant ½ cup lightly toasted pine nuts.

RED SWEET PEPPER AND TOMATO
Grill (broil) then skin 1 large sweet red pepper and, if you like the heat, ½ deseeded fresh red chilli pepper. Chop and mix with large peeled, deseeded and chopped tomato. Season with sea salt and freshly ground black pepper.

CREAMY MUSHROOM
Fry 125 g/4 oz/1½ cups washed and sliced button mushrooms in 15 g/½ oz/1 tbsp butter for 15–20 minutes, or until all the liquid which they produce has boiled away. Then stir in ½ tsp cornflour (cornstarch) and 125 ml/4 fl oz/½ cup single (light) cream. Stir well for about 2 minutes, until thickened, then remove from the heat. Season with sea salt and freshly ground black pepper, grated nutmeg and a squeeze of lemon juice.

lemony vegetables

One of my favourite vegetable dishes, and a great hit with my family this can be served as an accompanying vegetable, as a starter, or as a main course in its own right, perhaps with some cooked rice or a potato dish such as Light Gratin Dauphinois (page 38) or creamy mashed potatoes.

serves 4–6

225 g/8 oz broccoli
175 g/6 oz mangetouts
2 onions
2 sweet red peppers
1–2 fennel bulbs
2 leeks
90 ml/3 fl oz/$\frac{1}{3}$ cup olive oil
1 lemon
1 bayleaf
a good pinch of dried thyme
sea salt
freshly ground black pepper
chopped fresh parsley

First prepare the vegetables, all of which can be done in advance. Cut the thick stalks from the broccoli, then peel off the outer skin and cut the stalks into matchsticks. Separate the florets, halving any larger ones, so that they are all roughly the same size. Bring a large saucepan of water to the boil, put in the broccoli and blanch for 3 minutes, then drain into a colander and rinse under cold running water. Pat dry with kitchen paper and leave on one side.

Top and tail the mangetouts, and blanch these in the same way for 1 minute; drain, refresh under cold water and pat dry. Peel and slice the onions; deseed and slice the red peppers; trim and slice the fennel into eighths or sixteenths, depending on the size of the bulbs; clean, trim and slice the leeks into 2.5 cm/1 inch lengths.

When you are ready to make the dish, put the oil into a large saucepan or wok with the same quantity of water, the pared rind from half the lemon, the bayleaf and thyme. Put in the onions, red peppers, fennel and leeks and simmer for about 8 minutes, or until they are almost tender. Add the broccoli and mangetouts, and stir-fry for a further 2–3 minutes. Remove from the heat, add the grated rind of the other half of the lemon, and enough of the juice to give a pleasant tang. Season with salt and pepper, then serve, sprinkled with chopped parsley.

chestnut-stuffed mushrooms

I think these big, juicy mushrooms with their chestnut topping make a lovely festive dish. You can use either fresh, canned or vacuum-packed chestnuts. You will need about 450 g/1 lb fresh chestnuts to give the quantity used below.

Set the oven to 150°C/300°F/Gas 2. Stamp circles in the bread with a large pastry cutter; spread on both sides with butter and put them on a baking sheet. Bake for 1 hour, or until completely crisp and golden. Cool. These will keep in a tin for a few days.

To prepare the mushrooms, cut off any stems so that the surface is level, then wash the mushrooms and pat them dry on kitchen paper. Fry on both sides in the olive oil; drain well. Season with salt and pepper; set aside.

Melt the butter in a medium-large saucepan. Add the onion and fry for about 7 minutes, until soft. Chop up any pieces of mushroom stem, add these and cook for a minute or two longer. Remove from the heat and add the cooked chestnuts, breaking them up a bit as you do so to make a mixture which holds together but has some chunky bits in it. Add a dash of fresh lemon juice, and salt, pepper and grated nutmeg to taste.

To serve the dish, set the oven to 200°C/400°F/Gas 6 or preheat the grill (broiler) to high. Put the croûtes on a baking sheet or in a shallow casserole, then place a mushroom, black side up, on each one. Spoon the stuffing mixture on top. Cook until heated through – about 10 minutes under the grill (broiler), 15–20 minutes in the oven.

serves 4

8 large open mushrooms
olive oil for frying

for the stuffing:
25 g/1 oz/2 tbsp butter
1 large onion, peeled and finely chopped
350 g/12 oz/2 cups whole cooked chestnuts
fresh lemon juice
sea salt
freshly ground black pepper
grated nutmeg

for the croûtes:
8 slices of wholewheat bread
about 50 g/2 oz/5 tbsp soft butter

festive red cabbage

This is a useful dish because it cooks slowly and won't spoil if you cook it too long or keep it waiting. It also adds a moistness to the meal which often avoids the need for a separate sauce – and it's delicious, especially if you reheat it the next day.

serves 4–6

900 g/2 lb red cabbage
50 g/2 oz/4 tbsp butter
2 large onions, peeled and sliced
150 ml/5 fl oz/²/₃ cup red wine
150 ml/5 fl oz/²/₃ cup vegetable stock or water
sea salt
freshly ground black pepper
pinch of sugar
2–4 cloves garlic, peeled and crushed

Shred the cabbage, discarding the tough core. Melt half the butter in a large saucepan or casserole and fry the onions for about 5 minutes, then put in the cabbage and stir well, to coat it thoroughly with the butter.

Pour in the wine and stock, and add a teaspoonful of salt. Bring to the boil, then either cover, turn the heat right down and cook for about 1 hour on top of the stove, or cover and cook in the oven preheated to 170°C/325°F/Gas 3 for about 1½ hours. The cabbage should be very tender.

Mix the rest of the butter with the crushed garlic and add to the cabbage, along with salt, pepper and a pinch of sugar to taste.

VARIATION

Try a Nordic version of this cabbage, too: add chopped apples and spices and take out the garlic.

tagliatelle with creamy walnut sauce

This is a lovely pasta dish to make at Christmas when there are good walnuts around. Get some help on cracking them – or use really fresh shelled ones.

Fill a large saucepan two-thirds full of water, add the oil and bring to the boil.

Meanwhile, prepare the sauce. Grind the walnuts and garlic in a food processor and gradually add the cream and some salt and pepper.

When the water boils, add the pasta, give it a quick stir, then leave to cook for about 6 minutes, or according to package instructions. Don't let it get soggy. As soon as it's just done, drain it gently, add the butter and some salt and pepper, stirring very gently with a fork.

Add the sauce, mix quickly and lightly, and serve immediately on warmed plates. Serve Parmesan cheese separately for those who want it; it's best grated straight on to the hot pasta.

serves 4

1 tbsp olive oil
450 g/1 lb tagliatelle or fettuccine
15 g/^{1}/$_2$ oz/1 tbsp butter
freshly grated Parmesan cheese – optional

for the sauce:
225 g/8 oz walnuts in their shells, or 125–140 g/4–5 oz/1^1/$_3$–1^1/$_2$ cups shelled walnuts
1 clove garlic, peeled
150 ml/5 fl oz/^{2}/$_3$ cup whipping cream
sea salt
freshly ground black pepper

santa's sacks

Many other ingredients could be used with the potatoes for the filling here instead of sweetcorn and peanuts – I've used this combination because it's unfailingly popular with the kids I know. A can of chick peas (garbanzo beans), well drained, is good instead of sweetcorn, or chopped fried mushrooms, cheese or chopped nuts.

makes 8

8 sheets of filo pastry
4–6 tbsp olive oil

for the filling:
1 onion, peeled and chopped
1 tbsp olive oil
4 tbsp water
350 g/12 oz potatoes, peeled and cut into small dice
50 g/2 oz/¼ cup frozen sweetcorn kernels
50 g/2 oz/scant ½ cup salted peanuts
sea salt
freshly ground black pepper

First make the filling. In a medium-sized saucepan, fry the onion gently in the oil, with a lid on the pan, for 5 minutes. Add the diced potatoes, give them a stir, then cover and cook for 5 minutes. After that, put in the water, stir and cover, then cook until the potatoes are tender – about another 5–10 minutes. Take the pan off the heat and stir in the sweetcorn, peanuts and seasoning to taste.

Set the oven to 200°C/400°F/Gas 6. To make the sacks, take a piece of filo pastry and cut it into two 15 cm/6 inch squares. Keep the rest covered with cling film or a damp cloth to prevent it from drying out. Brush one of the squares with oil, then put the second one on top and brush with oil again. Put a good spoonful of the filling mixture in the middle, then dampen the edges with water and draw them up together, to make a sack. Brush the outside of the sack all over with more oil and put it on to a baking sheet. Continue like this until you have used up all the filling. Any filo pastry which is left over can be put back in its wrappings – it will keep well in the fridge for at least a month if it's well sealed.

Bake the sacks for about 20 minutes, or until they are crisp and golden all over, then serve at once.

oyster mushroom risotto

This makes a soothing and welcome meal at Christmas. It's easy to make and needs only a simple salad – sliced lettuce hearts, or tomatoes, for instance – to accompany it.

Melt 50 g/2 oz/4 tbsp of the butter in a large saucepan, add the onion and garlic and fry for 10 minutes, without browning. Put in the rice, some salt and the wine, then gradually add the water, mixing after each addition so that it moistens the rice each time and bring to the boil. The mixture should cook for about 20 minutes in all.

Melt the remaining butter in another pan, stir in the oyster mushrooms, and add these, too, to the mixture. Bring back to a simmer, then leave the rice to cook for a further 15 minutes, stirring it often as the liquid is absorbed, to prevent it from sticking. The risotto is done when it is creamy in consistency, without any excess liquid, and the rice is tender. If the liquid is absorbed before the rice is quite done, either put a lid on the pan and leave it off the heat for 10–15 minutes, or add a little more liquid and continue to simmer it gently for a few more minutes. Season with salt and pepper and serve with grated Parmesan cheese.

serves 2–3 as a main course

75 g/3 oz/6 tbsp butter
1 large onion, peeled and chopped
1 clove garlic, peeled and crushed
300 g/10 oz/1½ cups arborio rice
150 ml/5 fl oz/⅔ cup white wine – or use extra water
1 litre/1¼ pints/1 quart water or stock
125 g/4 oz oyster mushrooms
sea salt
freshly ground black pepper

to serve:
grated Parmesan cheese

father christmas faces

These can be made on lots of different bases, but I use soft white or brown rolls, which are about 10 cm/4 inches across. Cut them in half and toast them, then cover the entire surface with home-made tomato sauce, or very finely chopped deseeded tomatoes seasoned with sea salt and freshly ground black pepper. Then put a layer of grated Italian mozzarella cheese around the top to make hair and fur, and around the base to make a beard — you'll need about 125 g/4 oz/1 cup cheese.

Cut almost-halves of small black olives and position for shiny eyes, a piece of sweet red pepper, cut curvy, for the mouth, and a round of it for the nose and a final slice or two above the cheese for his hat. Make some of the cheese into eyebrows.

Grill (broil) just to heat through — not too much or the cheese will melt too much and brown, and the effect will be lost.

VARIATION
If you don't have any mozzarella, other white cheese, such as Wensleydale or Lancashire could be used, coarsely grated.

kate's butterbean croquettes

My daughter Kate invented this dish, which is very simple to make and very popular with kids. It's very quick to whizz up too – but it also freezes well. You can add spices, such as a teaspoonful of cumin seeds and ground coriander fried with the onion; or a dash of tomato chutney or chopped parsley, mixed in with the beans. They're good hot with Cranberry Sauce (page 21) or mango chutney; or cold, with yogurt and fresh herbs.

Heat the 2 tsp oil in a large saucepan, add the onion and fry, with a lid on the pan, for about 10 minutes, or until it is tender and lightly browned. Remove the pan from the heat. Drain the butterbeans and discard the liquid; add the butterbeans to the pan, mashing them with a spoon or with a potato masher to make a lumpy mixture which holds together. Season with salt and pepper as necessary.

Divide the mixture into eight pieces, form into croquette shapes and coat in dried wholewheat breadcrumbs. Arrange them on a greased baking sheet. When you're ready to bake the croquettes, put them into an oven preheated to 200°C/400°F/Gas 6 and bake them for about 30 minutes, or until they are brown and crisp on the outside, turning them over after about 20 minutes.

makes 8 croquettes to serve 4

2 tsp olive oil, plus extra
for greasing
1 onion, peeled and
chopped
2 x 425 g/15 oz cans
butterbeans
sea salt
freshly ground black pepper
dried wholewheat
breadcrumbs

flaky mushroom christmas tree

serves 4–6

350 g/12 oz frozen puff pastry, thawed
1 egg yolk, beaten with 1 tbsp water and a pinch of salt

for the filling:
25 g/1 oz/2 tbsp butter
1 onion, peeled and sliced
1 clove garlic, peeled and crushed
450 g/1 lb mushrooms, sliced
75 g/3 oz/1/2 cup cooked rice
75 g/3 oz/scant 1/2 cup cream cheese
1 tbsp chopped fresh parsley
1 tsp grated lemon rind
2–3 tsp lemon juice
sea salt
freshly ground black pepper

To make the filling, melt the butter in a small saucepan. Add the onion and cook for 5 minutes, then add the garlic and mushrooms. Fry until the mushrooms are tender and any liquid which they produce has gone – this can take 30 minutes. Add the rice, cream cheese, parsley, lemon rind and juice, and salt and pepper, stirring to mix well. Chill.

Set the oven to 200°C/400°F/Gas 6. On a lightly floured board, roll out the pastry into a 30 x 40 cm/12 x 16 inch rectangle. Cut in half to give two 30 x 20 cm/12 x 8 inch rectangles. Lay one half on top of the other and cut into a triangular Christmas tree shape. Try not to press too hard or they'll stick together. Lift one of the 'trees' on to a dampened baking sheet. Spoon the filling on top, leaving a little gap – not more than 1 cm/1/2 inch – around the edges. Dampen the edges, then put the second tree on top, pressing the edges together to seal. Prick lightly, then decorate with little cut-out pastry shapes, stuck on with cold water: a tiny angel or a star on the top, more little stars, hearts, teddy bears, crescents, crackers, or whatever, all over. You can also write HAPPY XMAS diagonally across it, if you have the patience to cut the letters. Brush with egg yolk, salt and water and bake for 30 minutes, or until the pastry is nicely browned. Serve piping hot, with the sauce.

cream and herb sauce

Put the cream and lemon juice into a small pan and stir gently until hot. Add the seasoning and herbs, and serve.

150 ml/5 fl oz/^{2}/$_3$ cup
double (heavy) cream
1 tbsp lemon juice
sea salt
freshly ground black pepper
1 tbsp chopped fresh herbs
– parsley, chives, tarragon

avocado with curried brazil nut stuffing

These hot avocados make a good quick lunch or supper. They are quite rich, so go well with something plain and low in fat – like brown rice cooked so that it's nice and fluffy, with a few fresh herbs added.

serves 4

2 large ripe avocados
juice of 1 lemon
6–8 spring (green) onions
1 tbsp olive oil
2 tsp curry powder
125 g/4 oz/scant 1 cup
Brazil nuts, chopped
sea salt
freshly ground black pepper
chilli powder

Halve the avocados and remove the stones. Using a teaspoon, scoop out the flesh without damaging the skin. Cut the flesh into rough chunks, put them into a bowl and add enough lemon juice to coat the pieces.

Next, wash and trim the onions, then slice finely. Heat the oil in a medium saucepan, add the onions and curry powder and fry over a gentle heat for 4-5 minutes, or until the onions are tender. Remove from the heat and add the avocado, chopped nuts, salt and pepper to taste, and a pinch or two of chilli to give it as much kick as you wish.

Heat the grill (broiler). Stand the avocado skins on a grill (broiler) pan or flameproof dish, spoon the Brazil nut mixture into the skins and grill (broil) for 5–10 minutes, or until the filling is heated through and the top is lightly browned.

shopper's delight

First make the garlic sauce by putting the soured cream or yogurt into a small saucepan with the garlic and salt and pepper to taste. Leave on one side.

Finely shred the lettuce, and keep that on one side, too. Halve the pitta breads through the middle so that each one makes two pockets. Put these under the grill (broiler) to warm through, but don't toast them.

Meanwhile, heat the oil in a large saucepan, add the leek, cabbage, mushrooms and green pepper and stir-fry for about 2 minutes, or until heated through. Gently heat the soured cream or yogurt and garlic, without letting it get anywhere near boiling.

Now fill the pitta pockets: put in a spoonful of shredded lettuce, then plenty of the stir-fried vegetables. Top with a good spoonful of the warm garlic sauce and finish with some more lettuce. Eat at once.

serves 4

$^1/_4$ **iceberg lettuce**
4 wholewheat pitta breads
2 tsp olive oil
125 g/4 oz/1 cup leek,
finely sliced
125 g/4 oz/2 cups cabbage,
finely shredded
125 g/4 oz/1$^1/_4$ cups button
mushrooms, sliced
125 g/4 oz/1 cup sweet
green pepper, sliced

for the garlic sauce:
150 ml/5 fl oz/$^2/_3$ cup
soured cream or Greek
yogurt
1–2 cloves garlic, peeled
and crushed
sea salt
freshly ground black pepper

christmas couscous

The vegetable stew part of this recipe is best made in advance and reheated, as the flavours improve – it is particularly good after freezing. Serve with small bowls containing harissa sauce, raisins, Greek yogurt, toasted pine nuts and cooked drained chick peas.

serves 6

50 g/2 oz/4 tbsp butter
450 g/1 lb onions, sliced
450 g/1 lb carrots, sliced
700 g/1½ lb butternut
squash, peeled and diced
1 tsp ground ginger
½ tsp ground cinnamon
½ tsp turmeric
¼–½ tsp white pepper
900 ml/1½ pints/3¾ cups
water or vegetable stock
450 g/1 lb courgettes
(zucchini), sliced
450 g/1 lb frozen broad
(fava) beans or sweetcorn
sea salt
squeeze of lemon juice
chopped fresh coriander
(cilantro)
450 g/1 lb couscous
1 tbsp olive oil
600 ml/1 pint/2½ cups
boiling water

Make the stew. Melt the butter in a large saucepan. Add the onions and fry for 5 minutes then add the carrots, squash and spices. Cook for a further 10 minutes, with a lid on, stirring from time to time, until all the vegetables are buttery and spicy. Add the water or stock and simmer for 10–15 minutes or until the vegetables are just becoming tender. Add the courgettes (zucchini) and beans or sweetcorn and cook for a further 5 minutes or so. Season with salt and lemon juice.

Cook the couscous according to package instructions, or put it into a large saucepan with the olive oil and boiling water. Cook gently for 5 minutes until it's fluffy and all the water has gone. Set aside.

Ladle the stew over the couscous and garnish with chopped fresh coriander. Serve with the bowls of extras at the table.

Christmas 'parties' cover a host of different occasions, ranging from simple nibbles with drinks to a buffet-style meal. This chapter includes a variety of recipes to enable you to cope with all the very different festive entertaining you are likely to do. There are simple dips and savouries, as well as more substantial 'centrepiece' dishes and salads, and some festive drinks – and don't forget to check other sections too. There are light savouries, which are good for drinks parties, in Lunches, Suppers and Snacks, and some of the main courses in Christmas Dinners could make very effective dishes for a buffet or fork supper.

One of the main problems when catering for a party is to know how much food to make. I generally think in terms of individual portions – how much any one person would reasonably eat. For a drinks party, I think about five or six little savouries per person is about right, and it's nice if some of these are hot and some cold. Quite a few of the recipes I've given here can be made in advance and frozen, then cooked or heated and served with dips, crudités, crisps and small savoury crackers or biscuits, for a relaxed, hassle-free occasion. Along with the food, allow about half a bottle of wine per person, or the equivalent in other drinks, plus some non-alcoholic drinks as well.

A buffet or fork supper can be as simple or as elaborate as you want to make it. I think it's best to serve a choice of at least two main courses (most people will have a little of each, so allow for this when you calculate quantities), plus three or four salads and/or vegetables, of which people will have only a spoonful or so. One golden rule, when estimating amounts I've found, is that a group of people never, for some reason, eat as much salad as they would at a smaller gathering. Again, if you think in terms of what one person would eat and multiply up by the number of guests, you'll be on the right track.

I haven't given separate pudding recipes in this section, although no real buffet is complete without one or two. There is, however, a whole range of spectacular and suitable offerings in Festive Puddings.

sweet red pepper and garlic dip

serves 6–8 as a first course

2 large sweet red peppers
6 large cloves garlic, peeled
150 ml/5 fl oz/²⁄₃ cup light olive oil
1–2 tbsp lemon juice
sea salt
freshly ground black pepper
25–50 g/1–2 oz/½–1 cup soft white breadcrumbs – optional

Quarter the red peppers, removing the stems and seeds, then put into a saucepan with the garlic and water just to cover. Bring to the boil, then simmer for about 15 minutes, or until the peppers are very tender. Drain well and leave until cold.

Put the peppers and garlic into a food processor and purée, gradually adding the oil and lemon juice to make a soft, creamy mixture like mayonnaise. Season, then chill before serving.

The dip will thicken slightly as it stands, but if you wish you can thicken it a bit more by stirring in some breadcrumbs. Add these gradually, allowing them several minutes to swell and thicken the mixture before adding more.

hummus

This is a useful dip to have at Christmas, or almost any time, and makes a good creamy vegan salad dressing, too. Be sure to get the deliciously mild pale golden-beige tahini, not the dark brown one. It keeps for ages.

Drain the chick peas (garbanzo beans), keeping the liquid. Put the chick peas into a food processor with the garlic and whizz to a thick purée, scraping down the sides as necessary. Add the tahini, oil, a tablespoonful of the lemon juice and a little of the reserved liquid, and whizz again. Keep on adding the reserved liquid until you have a smooth, creamy consistency, like lightly whipped cream. Taste the mixture and add more lemon juice if necessary, then season with salt and pepper.

To serve, spoon the hummus into a bowl, swirl a little olive oil on top and sprinkle with paprika.

serves 4 as a first course

425 g/15 oz can chick peas (garbanzo beans)
1 clove garlic, peeled
2 tbsp tahini
5 tbsp olive oil
juice of 1 lemon
sea salt
freshly ground black pepper

to serve:
olive oil
paprika

avocado dip

Just about everyone's favourite, this is very easy to whizz up, and makes a lovely dressing for salad too.

serves 4–6

1 large ripe avocado
1 tomato
1 small green chilli pepper
– optional
1–2 cloves garlic, peeled
and crushed
juice of 1 lime or lemon
sea salt
freshly ground black pepper

Halve the avocado, then remove the stone (pit) and peel. Mash the flesh roughly with a fork, or whizz it in a food processor if you want a thinner, creamier texture. Peel, deseed and chop the tomato and add to the mixture.

Deseed and finely chop the chilli, if you're using this, and add it to the avocado, being careful to wash your hands afterwards. Add the garlic and enough lime or lemon juice to give the dip a good tang, and season with salt and pepper. Serve as soon as possible.

This dip looks nice garnished with a leaf or two of fresh coriander (cilantro) or flatleaf parsley, a sprinkling of paprika pepper or a thin slice of lime or lemon.

baba ghanoush

Cut the aubergines (eggplants) in half and place them, cut side down, under a hot grill (broiler) for about 20 minutes until the skin is charred and the flesh feels soft. Leave them to cool, then remove the skin – it comes off very easily.

Put the flesh into a food processor with the garlic, oil and a couple of tablespoons of lemon juice, and whizz to a smooth, creamy purée. Taste and season, adding more lemon juice and the red wine vinegar as necessary, to give a good piquant flavour.

Spoon the mixture into a small bowl and serve sprinkled with chopped fresh parsley and garnished with some black olives.

serves 4

3 medium-sized aubergines
(eggplants)
1 clove garlic, peeled
3 tbsp olive oil
juice of 1–2 lemons
sea salt
freshly ground black pepper
2–3 tsp red wine vinegar

to serve:
chopped fresh parsley
black olives

mascarpone and herb dip

A rich and creamy dip for a party. You could make a less rich version by using curd cheese or, even less calorific, a skimmed milk smooth white cheese. Serve surrounded by crudités: radishes, baby sweetcorn, celery stalks, cauliflower florets, etc.

serves 4–6

250 g/9 oz/ heaping 1 cup
mascarpone cheese
3–4 tbsp plain yogurt
2 cloves garlic, peeled and
crushed
1 tsp grated onion
1–2 tbsp chopped fresh
chives
1–2 tbsp chopped fresh
parsley
Tabasco
sea salt
freshly ground black pepper

Put the mascarpone into a bowl, add the yogurt, garlic and onion and beat until creamy. Add the chives, parsley, a few drops of Tabasco to taste, and some salt and pepper. Chill until needed.

crostini

These delicious crisp croûtons with their colourful toppings are very useful for parties. In keeping with the occasion, they can be hearty, in true Tuscan style, or delicate, depending on the size of the bases.

A fairly slim French stick (baguette), sliced into rounds a bit less than 1 cm/½ inch thick, makes good, average-sized crostini; for mini ones, you can use very small bread rolls, such as bridge rolls, similarly sliced, to make smaller rounds. Put the rounds on baking sheets and put them in a coolish oven, 140–150°C/275–300°F/Gas 1–2, for about 20–30 minutes, or until they are dry and crisp. Half way through this process, brush on both sides with olive oil, then put back into the oven to finish crisping. Let them cool on the baking sheets.

For the toppings, you can use black olive pâté; a smooth soft goat's cheese and Swiss vegetable pâté, garnished with small sprigs of fresh herbs; pine nuts, capers, small pieces of grilled (broiled) sweet red pepper, or olives.

They're best assembled as near as possible to the time you're going to eat them so that the base remains crisp, but all the different parts, including the garnishes, can be prepared in advance.

goat's cheese balls

makes about 15

2 tbsp finely chopped fresh
chives
2 tbsp finely grated
hazelnuts or roasted cashew
nuts
1–2 tbsp paprika
450 g/1 lb medium-fat soft
goat's cheese

Have three plates, one each for the chives, nuts and paprika. Break off small pieces of cheese – about the size of a marble – and divide them among the three plates. Roll them to coat the outside and form a smooth ball.

Chill, then serve piled up on a small plate.

red and green sweet peppers

Cut the peppers into quarters, down from the stems. Place them, skin side up, under a very hot grill (broiler) for about 15–20 minutes until the skin has blackened and blistered. As one area of the pepper gets blackened, turn them so that all the shiny skin gets done.

Remove from the grill (broiler) and put them into a plastic bag, or between two plates, and leave them to get cold. Peel off the charred skins and rinse the peppers under cold water. Blot dry.

Cut the peppers into long thin pieces and put them into a shallow dish. Sprinkle them with lemon juice, oil and salt and pepper to taste. Leave them for a few hours if possible to allow the flavours to mellow and blend, giving them a stir from time to time. Check the seasoning, then sprinkle with parsley before serving.

serves 6–8 as a first course

**6 large juicy sweet peppers
– 3 red and 3 green
juice of 1 lemon
4 tbsp olive oil
sea salt
freshly ground black pepper
chopped fresh parsley**

imam bayildi

serves 6 as a first course or 2–3 as a light main course

6 baby aubergines (eggplants)
1 tbsp olive oil
1 medium-sized onion, peeled and finely chopped
1 clove garlic, peeled and crushed
2 tomatoes, peeled, deseeded and chopped
3 tbsp pine nuts
1 tbsp chopped fresh parsley
dash of lemon juice
sea salt
freshly ground black pepper

to garnish:
pine nuts

Cut the aubergines (eggplants) in half, leaving the stems on. With a small sharp knife and a teaspoon, carefully scoop out the flesh without breaking the skins. Set the skins aside. Chop the flesh. In a saucepan, heat the oil and fry the onion for 5 minutes, with a lid on the pan. Add the chopped flesh, garlic and tomatoes, cover and cook for a further 10–15 minutes, or until tender and purée-like.

Set the oven to 180°C/350°F/Gas 4. Blanch the skins in boiling water for 2 minutes, drain well and place in a greased shallow ovenproof dish. Add the pine nuts, parsley and lemon juice to the aubergine (eggplant) mixture, season and pile into the skins. Cover and bake for 20 minutes, or until browned and cooked. Serve cold, sprinkled with pine nuts.

mushrooms with garlic herb cheese

These make a pleasant warm or hot appetiser for a party, or they can be served with a salad garnish and some good bread, as a first course. You need small mushrooms, but not the very tight button ones.

Wash the mushrooms, then remove the stems by pushing them first one way and then the other; they should come out quite easily. Rub the mushrooms with a little olive oil, then place them, open side down, on a grill (broiler) pan or baking sheet.

Grill (broil) them for about 5 minutes, or until they are tender, then turn them up the other way and fill the cavities with the cheese. This can be done in advance. Just before you want to serve the mushrooms, put them under a hot grill (broiler) to heat them through and melt and lightly brown the cheese.

Transfer them to a serving dish or individual plates, and serve hot or warm.

makes about 16; serves 3–4 as a first course

225 g/8 oz mushrooms
olive oil
145 g/5 oz/$^2/_3$ cup soft French garlic and herb cheese

broccoli and stilton quiche

This is a very good quiche which you can also make with Brie instead of Stilton.

serves 6

175 g/6 oz/1¼ cups plain wholewheat flour or a half-and-half mix of plain white (all-purpose) and wholewheat flour
½ tsp sea salt
75 g/3 oz/6 tbsp butter
1 egg yolk
1 tbsp cold water

for the filling:
225 g/8 oz broccoli florets
300 ml/10 fl oz/1¼ cups single (light) cream
3 egg yolks
sea salt
freshly ground black pepper
125 g/4 oz blue Stilton cheese, thinly sliced

Set the oven to 200°C/400°F/Gas 6.

First make the pastry. Put the flours, salt, butter and egg yolk into a food processor, whizz for a few seconds until the mixture looks like breadcrumbs, then add the water and whizz again, briefly, until the mixture forms a ball of dough. Or make the pastry in the usual way by putting the flours and salt into a bowl, rubbing in the butter with your fingertips, then adding the egg yolk and water to bind to a dough.

On a floured board, roll out the pastry as thinly as you can and press gently into a 23 cm/9 inch quiche pan or dish. Trim off the excess pastry, put a circle of greaseproof (waxed) paper in the base and weigh it down with some crusts or dried beans (pulses). Bake the case for 7 minutes, then take out the paper and crusts or beans (pulses) and bake for a further 5–10 minutes, until the pastry base looks golden and feels set and firm.

To make the filling, boil the broccoli in a saucepan for 2–3 minutes, or until it is just tender. Drain immediately into a colander, then rinse under cold running water. Turn the broccoli on to a double layer of kitchen paper and blot dry. Put the broccoli and the Stilton into the pastry case. Beat together the cream and egg yolks, season and pour into the quiche.

Put into the oven, turn the heat down to 180°C/350°F/Gas 4 and bake for 30–40 minutes until set.

celebration wild rice with lemon mayonnaise

This is a pleasing mixture of flavours and textures; the chewiness and slightly smoky taste of wild rice is enhanced by the intensely flavoured porcini mushrooms, and the delicate, buttery avocado makes a complete contrast.

Put the rice into a saucepan with its height again in cold water and bring to the boil; let it simmer for about 45 minutes, or until it is tender and some grains have split open.

Meanwhile, wash the porcini and put them into a saucepan with water to cover. Bring to the boil, then take off the heat and leave to steep for 30 minutes. After that, simmer the porcini gently for about 15 minutes, or until they are tender and all the water has been absorbed. Drain the rice and put into a bowl, then add the porcini.

Now make the lemon mayonnaise. Mix together the yogurt, cream and mayonnaise, then stir in the lemon juice, adding it a little at a time and tasting the mixture to get the right amount of sharpness. Season with salt and freshly ground black pepper.

Halve the avocados and remove the stones (pits) and peel, then dice the flesh. Sprinkle the avocados with the lemon juice, and add these, and any extra juice, to the wild rice, along with the chopped chives. Season to taste with salt and freshly ground black pepper. Serve at once with the lemon mayonnaise, or cover and refrigerate for up to an hour before serving. Just before serving, add the nuts.

You can prepare this salad well in advance if you wish, as long as you leave out the avocado and nuts which should be added as near serving time as possible.

serves 8–10 at a party

225 g/8 oz/heaping 1 cup **wild rice**
25 g/1 oz/1 cup dried **porcini mushrooms**
2 ripe **avocados**
juice of 1 lemon
2 tbsp chopped fresh **chives**
125 g/4 oz/scant 1 cup **whole roasted cashew nuts, pine nuts or macadamia nuts**

lemon mayonnaise:
150 ml/5 fl oz/²/₃ cup **plain yogurt**
150 ml/5 fl oz/²/₃ cup **soured cream**
4 rounded tbsp good-**quality bottled mayonnaise**
juice of 1 lemon
sea salt
freshly ground black pepper

gnocchi alla romana

Although gnocchi alla romana is usually served as a first course, I think it makes a delicious vegetarian main course, especially when accompanied by some grilled (broiled) vegetables and perhaps some Italian Tomato Sauce (page 20). The gnocchi freeze excellently, either as separate cut shapes or assembled and sprinkled with Parmesan, ready for cooking.

serves 6

1 litre/1³/₄ pints/1 quart milk

1 bayleaf

200 g/7 oz/heaping 1 cup semolina

2 egg yolks

125 g/4 oz/1 cup Cheddar cheese, grated

sea salt

freshly ground black pepper

grated nutmeg

50 g/2 oz/¹/₂ cup Parmesan cheese, freshly grated

to serve:

chargrilled vegetables – opposite page

Put the milk and bayleaf into a large saucepan and bring to the boil. Add the semolina gradually in a thin stream, from well above the saucepan, stirring all the time. Bring the mixture to the boil, stirring, then let it cook gently for about 15 minutes until it is very thick. Remove from the heat and beat in the egg yolks and grated cheese. Season with plenty of salt, pepper and grated nutmeg. Spread the mixture out on an oiled baking sheet to a thickness of 1 cm/¹/₂ inch or a bit less, and leave to get cold and firm.

Cut the gnocchi mixture into shapes using a sharp pastry cutter, then assemble the dish. Put any odd shapes and trimmings onto a lightly greased shallow dish – a 30 cm/12 inch round ceramic pizza plate is ideal. Top with the remaining shapes and sprinkle generously with the Parmesan cheese. Grill (broil) until the top is golden brown and bubbling, and the inside heated through. Serve immediately, with chargrilled vegetables.

chargrilled vegetables

These can be grilled (broiled) before the gnocchi, as they can be served warm.

Remove the outer leaves from chicory (Belgian endive) and radicchio, then cut them downwards, halving the chicory (Belgian endive) and cutting the radicchio into sixths or eighths, depending on its size. Brush lightly with olive oil, then put the vegetables under a hot grill (broiler) until they are lightly charred and wilted, but still crunchy, turning them over to do both sides. Put them into a serving dish, sprinkle with salt and pepper, and pour a little more olive oil over them if you like. I like to serve them with some chunky lemon wedges.

little brie and hazelnut bakes

These are quick, easy and delicious. Serve them with a crisp, simple salad such as lettuce, cucumber and tomato, or chicory (Belgian endive), watercress and orange, or celery and apple. They're also good with lightly cooked vegetables such as green beans, and I love them with the bitter-sweet fruity flavour of the home-made Cranberry Sauce on page 21.

serves 3–4

350 g/12 oz Brie cheese
50 g/2 oz/scant ¹/₂ cup hazelnuts, skinned

Cut the Brie, including the rind, into 1 cm/¹/₂ inch chunky pieces and place them close together in a single layer in four individual ramekins, or in a shallow ovenproof dish. Chop the hazelnuts roughly – I give them a quick whizz in the food processor – and sprinkle evenly over the top.

Place under a hot grill (broiler) for about 10 minutes, until the Brie has heated through and half melted, and the nuts have toasted. Serve at once.

chunky hazelnut and tomato terrine

Set the oven to 200°C/400°F/Gas 6. Prepare a 450 g/1 lb loaf pan (measuring about 18 x 10 x 7.5 cm/6 x 4 x 3 inches). Put a long strip of non-stick paper across the base and up the two narrow sides.

Melt the butter in a medium-large saucepan, add the onion and fry for 7–8 minutes until soft but not browned, then add the mushrooms, tomatoes, garlic and basil and fry for a further 5 minutes.

Meanwhile, chop the hazelnuts coarsely. Add these to the mixture in the saucepan, along with the fresh breadcrumbs, chopped parsley, water or stock, soy sauce and lemon juice.

Mix well and season with salt and pepper, then spoon the mixture into the prepared pan and smooth the top level. Bake, uncovered, for about 40 minutes, or until the terrine feels firm to the touch. Leave it to cool completely in the pan, then chill. Serve cold, thinly sliced, with warm Garlic Sauce.

serves 8 at a party

25 g/1 oz/2 tbsp butter
1 onion, peeled and finely chopped
125 g/4 oz/1$\frac{1}{2}$ cups button mushrooms, chopped
2 tomatoes, peeled and chopped
1 clove garlic, peeled and crushed
1 tsp basil
200 g/7 oz/scant 1$\frac{1}{2}$ cups skinned hazelnuts
125 g/4 oz/2 cups fresh breadcrumbs
1 tbsp chopped fresh parsley
90 ml/3 fl oz/$\frac{1}{3}$ cup water or stock
2 tbsp soy sauce
1 tbsp lemon juice
sea salt
freshly ground black pepper

to serve:
warm Garlic Sauce – page 53

mushroom pâté with a herby crust

Cold and sliced, this makes a good pâté for a party – the Lemon Mayonnaise on page 67 goes very well with it, especially if you throw about a tablespoonful of green peppercorns into it. This pâté also makes a good first course and is an excellent sandwich filling, especially if you use a rather light granary bread.

serves 8 at a party

25 g/1 oz/2 tbsp butter
1 onion, peeled and chopped
700 g/1½ lb mushrooms
2 cloves garlic, peeled and crushed
50 g/2 oz/1 cup fresh breadcrumbs
1 egg
sea salt
freshly ground black pepper

for the herby coating:
butter
dried wholewheat crumbs
1½ tsp dried mixed herbs

Set the oven to 180°C/350°F/Gas 4. Line a greased 450g/1lb loaf tin with a long strip of nonstick paper to cover the base and narrow sides. Grease the paper and uncovered sides of the pan very generously with butter, then sprinkle thickly with dried wholewheat crumbs and 1 tsp of the mixed herbs, to form the herby coating.

To make the pâté, melt the butter in a large saucepan, add the onion and fry for 5 minutes, then add the mushrooms and garlic and fry for about 30 minutes or until all the liquid has gone. Whizz the mushroom mixture to a purée in a food processor, add the breadcrumbs and egg and whizz again briefly to mix.

Pour the mixture into the prepared pan and smooth the top level. Sprinkle the top quite thickly with dried crumbs, sprinkle with the remaining mixed herbs and dot with a little butter. Bake, uncovered, for about 40 minutes, or until the pâté feels firm to the touch, and a knife inserted in the middle comes out clean. Leave it to cool in the pan, then loosen the sides, turn the pâté out and strip off the paper. If you want a crisper coating, pop the pâté back into the oven for 10 minutes or so, or until the outside is crisp. Serve cold, thinly sliced.

mini chestnut
sausage rolls

These little 'sausages' are very popular with children. They freeze excellently too, and
can be baked from frozen – allow 5 minutes extra cooking time if you are doing this.
They are good served with a dip, such as yogurt and herb, soured cream and horseradish,
or with mango chutney.

First make the filling, by mixing together the chestnut
purée, onion, garlic, lemon juice, soy sauce, breadcrumbs
and chilli powder. Leave the mixture for a few minutes for
the breadcrumbs to thicken it, then add a few more if
necessary to make a soft mixture which you can roll into
sausages.

Set the oven to 190°C/375°F/Gas 5. On a lightly floured
board, roll out the pastry quite thinly, then cut across into
long strips about 5 cm/2 inches wide. Roll pieces of the
chestnut mixture into sausages about the width of a slim
little finger and the length of the pastry strips, and lay on
top of the pastry strips. Dampen the edges of the pastry
with cold water, then roll them round the chestnut
mixture, pressing the edges together. Prick the pastry with
a fork, then cut into 2.5 cm/1 inch lengths and place,
seam side down, on a baking sheet. Bake for about 10
minutes, or until the pastry is golden brown and crisp.

makes 48

**225 g/8 oz frozen puff
pastry, thawed**

for the filling:
**250 g/9 oz can
unsweetened chestnut
purée
1 small onion, peeled and
grated
1 clove garlic, peeled and
crushed
1 tbsp lemon juice
1 tbsp soy sauce
100 g/4 oz/2 cups soft
wholewheat breadcrumbs
good pinch of chilli powder**

party roulade

serves 6

50 g/2 oz/1 cup soft white
breadcrumbs
150 ml/5 fl oz/²/₃ cup
(light) single cream
2 tbsp water
175 g/6 oz/1¹/₂ cups
Gruyére cheese, grated
4 eggs, separated
sea salt
freshly ground black pepper
cayenne pepper
a little grated Parmesan
cheese for dusting

for the filling:
450 g/1 lb asparagus
2 tbsp lemon juice
2 tbsp olive oil
150 g/5 oz Lingot du Berry
or other similar medium-fat
soft goat's cheese
1 tbsp chopped fresh
parsley

Set the oven to 200°C/400°F/Gas 6. Line a 32 x 23 cm/13 x 9 inch Swiss (jelly) roll pan with non-stick paper.

Mix together the breadcrumbs, cream, water, cheese and egg yolks. Season with salt, pepper and a couple of pinches of cayenne.

Whisk the egg whites until stiff, then fold into the egg yolk mixture. Turn into the prepared pan, spreading it level into the corners. Bake for 10–15 minutes or until set and firm to a light touch. Leave in the pan and cover with a clean cloth that has been wrung out in warm water. Set aside to get completely cold.

To make the filling, trim the asparagus and cook until just tender; drain. Cut off the tips and chop the rest. Put it all in a shallow dish, sprinkle with the lemon juice and oil and season. Leave to get cold.

To assemble the roulade, sprinkle a large sheet of non-stick paper with grated Parmesan. Remove the cloth from the roulade and turn the roulade out on to the paper. Trim the edges. Spread the goat's cheese all over the roulade. Remove 6 tips from the asparagus and put the rest over the roulade, on top of the cheese – don't use the dressing which may remain with the asparagus. Sprinkle with the parsley.

Carefully roll up the roulade, using the paper to help. Place on a dish and garnish with the reserved asparagus tips, placed diagonally along the top.

mixed leaf salad

This is a mixture of radicchio, frisee, lamb's lettuce, some ordinary 'floppy' lettuce – not too much – rocket (arugula) and some freshly chopped herbs if available, especially tarragon and chives. I usually serve with a 'normal' vinaigrette, which I generally make with 1 tbsp wine vinegar to 3 tbsp olive oil, a good pinch of sugar, about ½ tsp Dijon mustard, preferably Grey Poupon, and some sea salt and freshly ground black pepper. Tear up the leaves, making sure there's a nice mix of colours, with plenty of red.

cucumber and dill salad

serves 4

1 large cucumber
1 small onion (optional)
sea salt
freshly ground black pepper
about ¹/₂ tsp sugar
1 tsp white mustard seeds
1 tbsp chopped fresh dill or
1 tsp dried dill weed
2 tbsp wine vinegar

Peel and thinly slice the cucumber and the onion, if you're using this. Put the slices into a shallow dish and sprinkle with a little salt, pepper and sugar. Mix in the mustard seeds, dill and vinegar, cover and leave until you need it.

The salad will make quite a lot of juice – that's normal. Drain it off before serving, or not, as you wish. It's nice mopped up with some bread.

lettuce heart salad
with fresh herb dressing

Wash the lettuces, taking off the outer leaves but keeping the hearts intact; then slice. Put the herbs, mustard, sugar, some salt and pepper and the vinegar into a salad bowl – a glass one is nice – and mix together. Gradually stir in the oil. Cross salad servers over the top of the dressing and put the lettuce in on top. Gently toss the lettuce in the dressing just before you serve the salad.

serves 3–4

2 hearty lettuces, such as
Little Gem
1 tbsp chopped fresh herbs
– tarragon is especially
good if you can get it,
otherwise chives or mint
$^1/_2$ tsp Dijon mustard
good pinch of sugar
sea salt
freshly ground black pepper
1 tbsp red wine vinegar
3 tbsp olive oil

green and orange salad

The juice from the oranges provides a light dressing for this refreshing salad, although you can add 1–2 tbsp of olive oil to make it into more of a vinaigrette-type of dressing if you prefer. Ruby oranges are particularly good if you can get them.

serves 4

2 chicory (Belgian endive)
4 small sweet oranges
75 g/3 oz/3 cups watercress

Wash the chicory (Belgian endive), cut it downwards into eighths and put it into a bowl. Holding the oranges over the bowl to catch the juice, cut away the peel and pith, then slice the orange flesh into thin circles. Add the watercress and toss all the ingredients together.

coleslaw

Coleslaw is so quick and easy to make, and the home-made version so good, that I wonder why people buy it ready-made.

Put the cabbage and carrots into a large bowl, together with any of the optional extras. Add the yogurt, mayonnaise and salt and pepper to taste and mix well. Sharpen with a little lemon juice if you like, before serving.

serves 6

450 g/1 lb white cabbage, finely shredded
225 g/8 oz carrots, scraped and coarsely grated
150 ml/5 fl oz/²/₃ cup low-fat plain yogurt
4 tbsp mayonnaise
sea salt
freshly ground pepper
lemon juice – optional

optional additions:
2 onions, peeled and finely sliced
1 small sweet green pepper, deseeded and chopped
125 g/4 oz/³/₄ cup raisins

watercress
and radish salad

This is an easy salad to make – and a pretty, festive combination of colours too. It tastes wonderfully fresh as it is, but if you prefer, you can serve it dressed with a light vinaigrette.

serves 4

125 g/4 oz/scant cup radishes

75 g/3 oz/3 cups watercress

Wash the radishes, and halve them or leave them whole, as you wish. Give the watercress a quick swish through cold water, then shake dry and put into a bowl with the radishes.

mulled wine

Scrub the oranges, then stick the cloves into one and put all of them into a stainless steel or enamel saucepan with the cinnamon stick, wine and liqueur. Heat gently to just below boiling, then keep at this temperature for 10–15 minutes. Taste and add a little sugar as necessary, then ladle into warmed glasses.

serves 4–6

5 oranges
5–6 cloves
1 cinnamon stick
1 bottle red wine
1 glass Cointreau or other orange liqueur
a little sugar to taste

mulled apple juice

Spices go well with apples, and this delightful, warming drink has something of the flavour of mulled wine, without any alcohol.

serves 6

1 litre/1¾ pints/1 quart still apple juice
1 orange
6 cloves
1 cinnamon stick
demerara sugar

Pour the apple juice into a saucepan. Stick the cloves into the orange, then slice it fairly thinly and add to the apple juice along with the cinnamon stick. Heat gently for about 30 minutes to draw out the flavour of the spices. Taste and add a little demerara sugar to taste, ladle into glasses and serve at once.

ginger punch

Wash, then thinly slice the lemons and oranges. Put them into a large bowl and add the mint, bruising it a bit with a spoon to help bring out the flavour. Sprinkle over the sugar and leave to chill for at least an hour or two, or until you're ready to serve the punch.

Mix in the ginger ale, soda water and ice cubes, and serve at once.

serves 10–12

3 lemons

3 oranges

6–8 sprigs of fresh mint

2 tbsp caster (superfine) sugar

1 l/1³/₄ pints ginger ale

1 l/1³/₄ pints soda water

12 ice cubes

sloe gin and tonic

This is such a lovely festive drink that I had to include it, although it does need some advance preparation – in September or October, to be exact. If you're too late, you can buy it, but do try making it next year as it's so warming and festive. You can drink it undiluted as a liqueur, as well as with tonic.

450 g/1 lb ripe sloes
70 cl bottle gin
125 g/4 oz/heaping ¹/₂ cup caster (superfine) sugar
a few drops of almond extract
tonic water, to serve

Wear an apron: the juice splatters and is indelible. Squish the sloes, or prick them with a darning needle, depending on how firm they are. Put them into a large empty plastic water bottle with the rest of the ingredients and shake. Leave for 2 months, shaking daily. Then strain twice through double muslin (cheese cloth). Serve with tonic water. For a party; make up a jugful with tonic water and ice.

The menus in this section are all for six people, although quantities can easily be reduced – sometimes individual recipes will make enough for six to have one serving hot and one cold, with salads and pickles. Except for the Moulded Rice with Two Sauces in menu 6, main courses can be made in advance and frozen, or made on Christmas Eve and kept overnight in the fridge – it's a great help to get the major dish done ahead of time. The same applies to the basic sauces: if you want plenty of time to enjoy Christmas Day, make and freeze these as I've explained on page 11. For dessert, I suggest something that can be taken care of in advance or something straightforward, like ice cream for the children or an exotic fruit salad – see the menus that follow for suggestions. All are served cold and benefit from being made in advance.

Christmas Pudding is an alternative to the desserts recommended in the menus – if the classic one is too heavy, try the Light Christmas Puddings on page 139. Much of the preparation for both of these can be done in advance.

I've suggested first courses, vegetables and accompaniments which I think go well with each of the main dishes given here and I've tried to avoid repetition, but do change the menus to suit your own taste. If you're cooking for only one or two vegetarians, just reduce the quantity; most of them will adapt well. Or you can serve the vegetarian main course as an extra dish to the general meal, which the meat-eaters can share.

Warm plates make such a difference, so don't forget to organise somewhere to warm them in advance of serving; the cool part of the oven or the warming drawer if you have one, a short cycle in the dishwasher, or even be ready to dip them quickly into very hot water before dishing out.

For all the menus I've given timetables for lunchtime Christmas dinner, which is what most families, including my own, seem to like best, but they could, of course, easily be adapted if you're planning an evening feast.

menu 1

Melon and Star Fruit Compôte

Cashew Nut Roast with Herb Stuffing
Roast Potatoes • Carrots with Parsley Butter
My Favourite Way with Brussels Sprouts
Vegetarian Gravy
Bread Sauce • Cranberry Sauce

Meringue Nests or
Chocolate or Vanilla Ice Cream

Mince Pies

Wines: Mâcon (white), Beaujolais (red)

melon and
star fruit compôte

A melon with greenish flesh looks good with the yellow star fruit – either an ogen melon, or a honeydew, for instance. These are best bought a few days before you need them, so that they can ripen up. I choose the yellowest star fruit that I can find.

Halve the melon, remove the seeds, then cut the flesh into pieces or scoop it out with a parisienne cutter (melon baller) to make balls. Put the melon into a bowl with the orange juice and a little honey to taste, as necessary. If the melon is sweet you probably won't need any honey.

Cut the star fruit across – like slicing a cucumber – to produce thin star-shaped pieces. Add to the compôte then divide the mixture between six bowls.

1 ripe melon
juice of 2 oranges
clear honey
1 large ripe star fruit
(carambola)

cashew nut roast

50 g/2 oz/4 tbsp butter
1 large onion, peeled and
sliced
225 g/8 oz/1³/₄ cups
unroasted cashew nuts
125 g/4 oz white bread,
crusts removed
2 large cloves garlic
200 ml/7 fl oz/scant 1 cup
water or light vegetable
stock
sea salt
freshly ground black pepper
grated nutmeg
1 tbsp lemon juice
1 quantity of Herb Stuffing
– opposite page

to garnish
sprigs of fresh parsley
small lemon slices

Set the oven to 200°C/400°F/Gas 6. Prepare a 450 g/1 lb loaf pan (measuring about 18 x 10 x 7.5 cm/6 x 4 x 3 inches). Put a long strip of non-stick paper across the bottom and up the two narrow sides, then use some of the butter to grease the pan and paper well.

Melt most of the remaining butter in a medium-sized saucepan, add the onion and fry for about 10 minutes until tender but not browned. Remove from the heat.

Grind the cashew nuts in a food processor with the bread and garlic, then add to the onion together with the water or stock, salt, pepper, grated nutmeg and lemon juice to taste.

Put half the cashew nut mixture into the prepared pan, top with the herb stuffing, then spoon the rest of the nut mixture on top. Dot with the remaining butter. Stand the pan in another pan to catch any butter which may ooze out, then bake for about 30 minutes or until firm and lightly browned. Cover the roast with foil if it gets too brown before then.

Cool for a minute or two in the pan, then slip a knife around the sides, turn the nut roast out and strip off the paper. Garnish with sprigs of parsley and small slices of lemon, and surround with roast potatoes, if you're serving them.

herb stuffing

Peel and grate the onion. Chop the parsley. Place the onion and parsley in a bowl and add the softened butter, dried thyme and marjoram. Season to taste with salt and pepper, then mix all the ingredients together well.

1 small onion
25 g/1 oz/$\frac{1}{2}$ cup fresh parsley
125 g/4 oz/2 cups white breadcrumbs
50 g/2 oz/4 tbsp softened butter
$\frac{1}{2}$ tsp each dried thyme and marjoram
sea salt
freshly ground black pepper

roast potatoes

1 kg/2 lb potatoes
light olive oil

Set the oven to 200°C/400°F/Gas 6. Peel the potatoes and cut them into halves. Put them into a saucepan, cover with water and parboil for 5 minutes, or until they are almost tender, but not showing any signs of breaking up.

When they are almost done, pour a thin layer of oil – 3 mm/⅛ inch – into a baking dish or roasting pan and put into the oven to heat. Drain the potatoes thoroughly and, standing well back, put them into the oil, which should be smoking hot and sizzle and splutter as you put them in. Turn them with a perforated spoon, then put into the top of the oven.

Have a look at the potatoes after about 20 minutes and, if they're doing well, turn them over and continue to cook gently, alongside the nut roast or other main course. They will keep happily at this temperature for 45–60 minutes.

Drain them well on kitchen paper before serving.

carrots with parsley butter

Scrub or peel the carrots, then cut them into circles or sticks. Put the carrots into a saucepan, cover with boiling water and bring back to the boil. Cover and cook for 5–10 minutes, or until they are just tender; don't let them get soggy.

Drain, add the butter, parsley, salt and pepper, and serve immediately.

700 g/1½ lb carrots
25 g/1 oz/2 tbsp butter
1–2 tbsp chopped fresh parsley
sea salt
freshly ground black pepper

my favourite way
with brussels sprouts

I like Brussels sprouts which are only just done, nice and crunchy and green. I find that the best way to achieve this is to cut them in half – a trick I learnt from my mother.

700 g/1¹/₂ lb Brussels
sprouts
25 g/1 oz/2 tbsp butter
sea salt
freshly ground black pepper

Remove the outer leaves from the sprouts, then wash them and halve them. Just before you want to serve the meal, bring 1 cm/¹/₂ inch of water to the boil in a large saucepan. Put in the sprouts, cover with a lid and boil for 4–5 minutes, or until they are just done. Drain and add the butter and salt and pepper.

vegetarian gravy

Heat the oil or butter in a saucepan and add the flour. Stir over a moderate heat for a few minutes until the flour turns nut-brown. Standing well back, pour in the water or stock and stir until slightly thickened. Simmer for 10 minutes, then add the soy sauce and a little seasoning to taste if necessary.

3 tbsp olive oil or melted butter
3 tbsp plain wholewheat flour
600 ml/1 pint/2^1/$_2$ cups water or stock
3 tbsp dark soy sauce
sea salt
freshly ground black pepper

FOR THE REMAINDER OF THE MENU
Bread Sauce page 22
Cranberry Sauce page 21
Meringue Nests page 145
Ice Creams pages 157 and 149
Mince Pies page 10

menu 1
countdown

MAKE IN ADVANCE

- Cashew Nut Roast: freeze uncooked, for 2–4 weeks.
- Vegetarian Gravy, Bread Sauce, Cranberry Sauce: all of these can be made in advance and frozen.
- Meringue Nests: cook and freeze the nests unfilled.
- Ice Cream: make up to 14 days ahead, cover well and freeze.
- Mince Pies: cook a batch and freeze – it's easier to have a cooked batch for heating through on Christmas Day.

CHRISTMAS EVE

- Remove from the freezer: Cashew Nut Roast, Vegetarian Gravy, Bread Sauce, Cranberry Sauce, Meringue Nests. Put the Mince Pies on to a serving dish. Leave everything to thaw overnight.
- Peel the potatoes and leave in a pan with cold water to cover. Prepare the sprouts and carrots; put them into separate plastic bags in the fridge.
- Get together serving dishes – a large one for the nut roast and potatoes; vegetable dishes for the sprouts and carrots; gravy boats/jugs/bowls for sauces; a round serving plate for the meringue. Gather plates for the first course, main course and pudding.

CHRISTMAS DAY

- 11.00 am Lay the table. This can be done on Christmas Eve if you're in the mood and don't need the table for breakfast. Chill the white wine. Make the fillings for the meringue and pile into the nests. Store in the fridge.

🕰 **11.15 am** Set the oven to 200°C/400°F/Gas 6. Prepare the Melon and Star Fruit Compôte; cover and chill in the fridge. Parboil the potatoes for about 5 minutes. Prepare the garnish for the nut roast.

🕰 **11.40 am** Heat the oil for potatoes at the top of the oven. Put the nut roast in towards the bottom of the oven. Put the potatoes into the oil and put back into the top of the oven.

🕰 **12.30 pm** Open the red wine. Turn the nut roast out on to its plate; cover loosely with foil and put back into the oven. Reheat the sauces, then serve them out and keep them warm at the bottom of the oven.

🕰 **12.45 pm** Put the water on for the carrots and sprouts. Cook until they are only just done, then drain, put them into warmed vegetable dishes in the bottom of the oven to keep warm.

🕰 **12.55 pm** Open the white wine; light the candles; put the ice cream into the fridge.

🕰 **1.00 pm** Dinner is served.

🕰 **After the starter** Quickly serve out the sauces if you haven't already done so. Lift the potatoes out on to kitchen paper with a perforated spoon; quickly blot off excess oil, then put them around the nut roast; garnish. Put the mince pies, covered in foil, into the oven towards the bottom to warm through. Take the main course dishes to the table.

🕰 **After the main course** Sprinkle the mince pies with sugar; take to the table with the pudding.

menu 2

Iced Melon Soup with Violets

Chestnut and Red Wine Pâté en Croûte
Horseradish Sauce • Vegetarian Gravy
Light Mashed Potatoes
Julienne of Root Vegetables

Rum-Macerated Fruits with Coconut and Lime Cream
or Chocolate or Vanilla Ice Cream

Mince Pies

Wines: Chardonnay (white) Côtes du Rhône
or Cabernet Shiraz (red)

iced melon soup with violets

Halve the melons and remove the seeds. Scoop out the flesh and whizz in the food processor until smooth, adding a little sugar if necessary. Chill in the fridge until ready to serve.

Serve the soup in chilled bowls, garnished with a few violet heads floating in each one. Or for extra effect, serve from one large bowl set over a larger bowl of crushed ice.

2 ogen melons, or 1 large honeydew melon
2 tbsp caster (superfine) sugar
small bunch of fresh violets, washed and very gently shaken dry

chestnut and red wine pâté en croûte

25 g/1 oz/2 tbsp butter

2 medium-sized onions, peeled and chopped

2 cloves garlic, peeled and crushed

50 g/2 oz/¹/₂ cup button mushrooms, sliced – optional

90 ml/ 3 fl oz/¹/₃ cup red wine

75 g/3 oz/1¹/₂ cups soft fresh white or brown breadcrumbs

¹/₂ x 350 g/12 oz can unsweetened chestnut purée, or mashed fresh, vacuum-packed or canned chestnuts

sea salt

freshly ground black pepper

450 g/1 lb frozen puff pastry, thawed

to glaze:

a little beaten egg

Melt the butter in a medium-large saucepan, add the onions and fry for about 10 minutes, until tender but not browned. Add the garlic and mushrooms, if you're using them, and cook for a further 2–3 minutes. Pour in the wine and let it bubble away for a minute or two until most of the liquid has gone; then remove from the heat and stir in the breadcrumbs, chestnut purée, and salt and pepper to taste.

Set the oven to 230°C/450°F/Gas 8. On a lightly floured board, roll out the pastry into two strips, one measuring about 15 x 30 cm/6 x 12 inches; the other 22 x 30 cm/9 x 12 inches. Put the smaller strip on to a baking sheet brushed with cold water. Spoon the chestnut mixture on to the pastry, keeping 1 cm/¹/₂ inch clear all round the edges, and piling it up well into a nice loaf-like shape in the middle. Brush the edges of the pastry with cold water, then ease the second piece of pastry on top; press down lightly and trim the edges. Cut the trimmings into holly leaves, Christmas trees, bells or whatever you fancy, and stick them on top of the pastry with water. Make a few small steam holes, then brush with beaten egg if you're using this.

Put into the oven and bake for 7–8 minutes, then reduce the temperature to 200°C/400°F/Gas 6 and bake for a further 20–25 minutes.

light mashed potatoes

Peel the potatoes and cut into even-sized pieces, not too big. Put them into a saucepan, cover with water and boil until they are tender, about 15 minutes. Drain them, keeping the liquid, then mash them thoroughly using a potato masher or by pushing them through a vegetable mill – not in the food processor, or you'll end up with glue. Add the butter, cream and enough of the reserved water to make a very light consistency, like lightly whipped cream. Season with salt and pepper and serve immediately.

VEGAN VERSION
Use 40 g/1½ oz/3 tbsp vegan margarine instead of the butter, and soya milk instead of the cream.

1 kg/2 lb potatoes
25 g/1 oz/2 tbsp butter
4 tbsp cream
sea salt
freshly ground black pepper

julienne of root vegetables

Choose a mixture of whatever root vegetables are available: some carrot gives a good basis, and kohlrabi adds a pleasant flavour if you can get it. Parsnip, swede (rutabaga) and celeriac (celery root) are other possibilities. Make sure that any alternative that you choose will cook in the same amount of time, or add the quicker-cooking vegetables, such as, for instance, courgette (zucchini) matchsticks, towards the end of the cooking time.

225 g/8 oz carrots
225 g/ 8 oz kohlrabi
225 g/8 oz turnips
25 g/1 oz butter
squeeze of lemon juice
sea salt
freshly ground black pepper
grated nutmeg

Scrub, scrape or finely peel the root vegetables, depending on their condition, then cut them into thin matchsticks. Cook them, covered in boiling water, or in a steamer, for 5 minutes, or until they are just tender.

Drain, then add the butter and lemon juice plus salt, pepper and nutmeg to taste. Serve immediately.

horseradish sauce

Mustard Sauce is a pleasant variation of this sauce; use a little Dijon or whole-grain mustard instead of the creamed horseradish. A teaspoonful of drained, pickled green peppercorns or capers make a pleasant, piquant addition too.

Mix the soured cream or yogurt with enough creamed horseradish to give the sauce a good tang; season with salt before serving.

300 ml/10 fl oz/1¼ cups soured cream or creamy plain yogurt
1–2 tbsp creamed horseradish
sea salt

FOR THE REMAINDER OF THE MENU

Vegetarian Gravy page 93
Rum-Macerated Fruits with Coconut and Lime Cream page 148
Ice Creams pages 157 and 149
Mince Pies page 10

menu 2
countdown

MAKE IN ADVANCE

- Chestnut and Red Wine Pâté en Croûte: freeze, uncooked, for 2–4 weeks.
- Vegetarian Gravy: make in advance and freeze.
- Ice Cream: make up to 14 days ahead, cover well and freeze.
- Mince Pies: cook a batch and freeze – it's easier to have a cooked batch for heating through on Christmas Day.

CHRISTMAS EVE

- Remove from the freezer: Chestnut and Red Wine Pâté en Croûte; sauces as required, including Vegetarian Gravy. Put the Mince Pies on to a serving dish. Leave everything to thaw overnight.
- Peel the potatoes and leave in a pan with cold water to cover. Prepare the root vegetables; put them into a plastic bag in the fridge. Make the Horseradish Sauce, spoon it into a serving bowl or jug, cover and keep in the fridge.
- Make the Coconut and Lime Cream, spoon into a bowl, cover and keep in the fridge.
- Get together serving dishes – a large one for the pâté; vegetable dishes for potatoes and root vegetables; gravy boats/jugs/bowls for sauces; a serving dish for the pudding. Gather plates for the first course, main course and pudding.

CHRISTMAS DAY

- **11.00 am** Lay the table. This can be done on Christmas Eve if you're in the mood and don't need the table for breakfast. Chill the white wine.

⏰ **11.45 am** Set the oven to 230°C/450°F/Gas 8. Put the potatoes on to boil. Prepare the soup, put it into a bowl, cover and chill. Prepare and marinate the fruit for the pudding.

⏰ **12.20 pm** Mash the potatoes and put into the warmed serving dish; cover and put into the oven.

⏰ **12.30 pm** Put the pâté into the oven. Open the red wine. Reheat the gravy, then serve out and keep warm at the bottom of the oven.

⏰ **12.38 pm** Turn the oven down to 200°C/400°F/Gas 6.

⏰ **12.45 pm** Put the water on for the root vegetables. Cook the vegetables until they are only just done, then drain and put into a warmed dish.

⏰ **12.50 pm** Pour the soup into bowls, garnish with the violets and take to the table.

⏰ **12.55 pm** Open the white wine; light the candles; put the ice cream into the fridge; check the pâté.

⏰ **1.00 pm** Dinner is served.

⏰ **After the first course** Quickly serve the vegetarian gravy and horseradish sauce if you haven't already done so. Lift the pâté en croûte on to a warmed plate. Put the mince pies, covered in foil, into the oven towards the bottom to warm through. Take the main course dishes to the table.

⏰ **After the main course** Sprinkle the mince pies with sugar; take to the table with the pudding.

menu 3

Cherry Tomatoes with Horseradish Cream

Stuffed Acorn Squash

Glazed Sweet Potatoes

Baby Sweetcorn and Mangetouts

Vegetarian Gravy • Port Wine Sauce

Cranberry Sauce

Lemon and Ginger Cheesecake

or Chocolate or Vanilla Ice Cream

Mince Pies

Wines: Semillon or Vouvray (white)

Cabernet Sauvignon or Merlot (red)

cherry tomatoes
with horseradish cream

Cover the cherry tomatoes with boiling water; leave for a few seconds until the skins have loosened, then drain and cover the tomatoes with cold water. Slip off the skins with a small sharp knife. Put the tomatoes into a bowl and season with a little salt, pepper and a pinch of sugar, if they need it. Chill until required.

Mix together the yogurt, mayonnaise and horseradish; season lightly and chill this, too.

Just before you want to serve this dish, put the tomatoes on to six individual serving dishes. Spoon the yogurt mixture over them and garnish with whole or shredded basil leaves.

450 g/1 lb cherry tomatoes
sea salt
freshly ground black pepper
pinch of sugar
4 tbsp plain yogurt
1 tbsp mayonnaise
1–3 tsp creamed
horseradish

to garnish:
fresh basil leaves

stuffed acorn squash

You can either use small acorn squash, allowing half for each person, or one bigger one, depending on what is available. I think small ones are particularly good, but the combination of firm, buttery squash and light nutty filling is delicious either way.

3 small squash – about
350–450 g/³/₄–1 lb each
25 g/1 oz/2 tbsp butter
1 onion, peeled and
chopped
1 small green chilli pepper
– optional
175 g/6 oz/heaping 1 cup
cashew nuts, lightly
chopped
3 tbsp desiccated
(shredded) coconut
1 tbsp chopped fresh
parsley
sea salt
freshly ground black pepper

Halve the squash, scoop out the seeds and trim the bases a little as necessary so that they stand level. Cook them in water to cover for about 15 minutes or until you can pierce the flesh easily with a knife. Drain well and blot with kitchen paper. Stand the squash in an ovenproof dish or on a baking sheet and season with a little salt and pepper.

Next make the filling. Melt half the butter in a saucepan, add the onion and fry for 10 minutes, letting it brown a bit. Meanwhile, halve the chilli, if you're using this, and rinse away the seeds under cold running water. Chop the chilli and add to the onion, along with the cashew nuts and coconut, and fry for a further 2–3 minutes. Season and pile the mixture into the squash. Cut the remaining butter into 6 pieces and put on top of the stuffing. Set the oven to 200°C/400°F/Gas 6.

Cover the whole dish or baking sheet with foil and bake the squash for about 15 minutes, or until heated through. Remove the foil and bake for a further 5–10 minutes, then serve immediately.

glazed sweet potatoes

Get the type with delicious golden flesh – they make a marvellous Christmas vegetable – much easier to do than roast potatoes.

Scrub the potatoes and cut into even-sized pieces, not too big. Put them into a saucepan, cover with water and boil until they are tender, 10–15 minutes. Drain them, cool and remove the skins.

Grease an ovenproof dish generously with half the butter, then put the sweet potato pieces in on top. Dot with the remaining butter and sprinkle with the sugar, lemon juice and a little salt. The sweet potatoes can be baked when it's convenient for you: they can wait in the fridge overnight, or you can keep them in the freezer.

Set the oven to 200°C/400°F/Gas 6 and bake for 40–50 minutes. Have a look at them after about 30 minutes and turn them if necessary, so that they are golden brown and glazed all over.

1 kg/2 lb sweet potatoes
25 g/1 oz/2 tbsp butter
25 g/1 oz/2 tbsp light
brown sugar
2 tbsp lemon juice
sea salt

baby sweetcorn and mangetouts

350 g/12 oz mangetouts
350 g/12 oz baby
sweetcorn
15 g/¹/₂ oz/1 tbsp butter
sea salt
freshly ground black pepper

Top and tail the mangetouts; just wash the sweetcorn. Fill a large saucepan two thirds full of boiling water.

Just before you want to serve them, throw the mangetouts and sweetcorn into the water – they should be covered and able to move around in it. Bring back to the boil and boil for about 1–2 minutes, or until they are just tender.

Drain immediately into a colander, put them into a warmed serving dish with the butter and a little salt and pepper, and serve immediately.

port wine sauce

This sauce goes well with other Christmas Savouries, such as Cashew Nut Roast with Herb Stuffing, Yuletide Ring and also the Chestnut and Red Wine Pâté en Croûte, so it's worth having in the freezer.

Heat the oil in a small saucepan, add the onion and fry for 10 minutes until it is tender but not browned. Pour in the red wine, bring to the boil, and leave to simmer, without a lid, for about 10 minutes, or until the mixture has reduced to 300 ml/10 fl oz/1¼ cups.

Put the cornflour (cornstarch) into a small bowl and mix to a thin paste with the port, then pour this into the wine mixture and stir briefly until it has thickened slightly. Taste the sauce, and add salt, pepper and a little redcurrant jelly or sugar as necessary.

Leave to one side until just before you want to serve the sauce, then quickly stir in the butter to make it glossy.

3 tbsp olive oil

1 onion, peeled and finely chopped

600 ml/1 pint/2½ cups red wine

1 tsp cornflour (cornstarch)

2–3 tbsp port

sea salt

freshly ground black pepper

1–2 tsp redcurrant jelly or sugar – optional

25 g/1 oz/2 tbsp butter, cut into pieces

FOR THE REMAINDER OF THE MENU
Vegetarian Gravy page 93
Cranberry Sauce page 21
Lemon and Ginger Cheesecake page 147
Ice Creams pages 157 and 149
Mince Pies page 10

menu 3
countdown

MAKE IN ADVANCE

- Stuffing for Acorn Squash: freeze, uncooked, for 2–4 weeks.
- Vegetarian Gravy, Port Wine Sauce, Cranberry Sauce: all can be made in advance and frozen.
- Ice Cream: make up to 14 days ahead, cover well and freeze.
- Mince Pies: cook a batch and freeze – it's easiest to have a cooked batch for heating through on Christmas Day.

CHRISTMAS EVE

- Remove from the freezer: Stuffing for Acorn Squash, Vegetarian Gravy, Port Wine Sauce, Cranberry Sauce. Put the Mince Pies on to a serving dish. Leave everything to thaw overnight.
- Peel and parboil the sweet potatoes. Put them into a well-greased shallow casserole and top with butter, sugar and lemon juice. Cover and leave in a cool place. Prepare the mangetouts and baby sweetcorn; put them into a plastic bag in the fridge. Parboil the squash, drain well and place on a baking sheet. Cover loosely with foil and leave in a cool place. Make the cheesecake, cover and put in the fridge.
- Get together serving dishes – a large one to hold the squash; one for the sweet potatoes; a dish for the mangetouts and sweetcorn; gravy boats/jugs/bowls for sauces; a plate for the cheesecake. Gather plates for the first course, main course and pudding.

CHRISTMAS DAY

⏰ **11.00 am** Lay the table. This can be done on Christmas Eve if you're in the mood and don't need the table for breakfast. Chill the white wine.

⏰ **11.30 am** Prepare the cherry tomatoes. Keep the tomatoes and sauce separate; chill.

⏰ **11.50 am** Set the oven to 200°C/400°F/Gas 6.

⏰ **12.10 pm** Put the sweet potatoes into the oven towards the top.

⏰ **12.20 pm** Spoon the stuffing into the squash and put into the oven if you're using a large one; otherwise wait until 12.40 pm. Open the red wine. Reheat the sauces, then serve them out and keep them warm at the bottom of the oven.

⏰ **12.45 pm** Put the water on for the mangetouts and sweetcorn. Cook until they are only just done, then drain; put them into the warmed vegetable dish and put them into the bottom of the oven to keep warm. Serve out the first course and take to the table, ready.

⏰ **12.55 pm** Open the white wine; light the candles; put the ice cream into the fridge.

⏰ **1.00 pm** Dinner is served.

⏰ **After the first course** Quickly serve out the sauces if you haven't already done so. Lift the squash on to a serving plate; serve out the sweet potatoes, unless you're taking them to the table in the casserole, which is much easier. Put the mince pies, covered in foil, into the oven towards the bottom to warm through. Take the main course dishes to the table.

⏰ **After the main course** Sprinkle the mince pies with sugar; take to the table with the puddings.

menu 4

Celery and Stilton Soup

Yuletide Ring with Parsley Stuffing Balls
Wild Mushroom and Madeira Sauce
Leeks Cooked in Spiced Wine
Cock's Comb Roast Potatoes • Carrot Purée

Exotic Fruit Salad and Passion Fruit and Lime Sorbet

Mince Pies

Wines: Fumé Blanc (white)
Rioja or Shiraz (red)

celery and stilton soup

If you're going to freeze this soup, don't add the cheese. This can be grated ready for adding, and frozen separately, to save time.

Remove and reserve any leaves from the celery stalks then chop the celery. Heat the oil in a large saucepan, add the onion and celery and fry gently, with the lid on the pan, for about 10 minutes, until tender but not browned. Add the water or stock, bring to the boil and let the soup simmer for about 30 minutes, or until the celery is completely cooked and soft.

Liquidize the soup and pour it back into the pan through a sieve (strainer) to remove any stringy bits. Heat the soup to boiling point, then remove from the heat and add the cheese and reserved celery leaves. Stir gently until the cheese has melted into the soup.

Quickly check the seasoning – you probably won't need much as Stilton cheese is quite salty – and serve in warmed bowls.

1 bunch of celery, or outside stalks from 2 bunches – about 450 g/1 lb in all
1 tbsp olive oil
1 onion, peeled and chopped
1.5 litres/2$\frac{1}{2}$ pints/6$\frac{1}{4}$ cups water or stock
150–175 g/5–6 oz/1$\frac{1}{4}$–1$\frac{1}{2}$ cups Stilton cheese, grated
sea salt
freshly ground black pepper

yuletide ring

This is a ring of golden lentils garnished with leaves and berries to look like a Christmas wreath, and filled with parsley stuffing balls.

125 g/4 oz/½ cup butter
450 g/1 lb/2¼ cups split red lentils
600 ml/1 pint/2½ cups water
2 bay leaves
2 large onions, peeled and finely chopped
4 garlic cloves, peeled and crushed
juice of 1 lemon
sea salt
freshly ground black pepper

to serve:
Parsley Stuffing Balls – opposite page
flat-leaf parsley
cranberries or cherry tomatoes

Use 25 g/1 oz/2 tablespoons of the butter to generously grease a 22–23 cm/9–9½ inch ring mould (1.2 litre/2 pint/5 cup capacity). Preheat the oven to 180°C/350°F/Gas 4.

Put the lentils into a non-stick saucepan with the water and bay leaves. Bring to the boil, then cover and leave to simmer gently for about 20 minutes or until the lentils are pale in colour and tender.

Meanwhile, melt the remaining butter in another saucepan, add the onions and garlic, cover and cook very gently for 10 minutes, until tender. Add the onions to the lentils along with the lemon juice and salt and pepper to taste.

Spoon the lentil mixture into the ring mould – it won't completely fill it – and level the top. Cover with foil and bake for 45 minutes. To serve, slip a knife round the edges to loosen, invert a plate over the top, then turn the mould out on to the plate. Put the parsley stuffing balls into the centre and decorate the ring with some flat-leaf parsley leaves and whole cranberries or slices of cherry tomato.

mushroom pâté

Wash the mushrooms and chop them roughly. Melt the butter in a large saucepan, add the mushrooms and fry them without a lid on the pan – they will soon make a great deal of liquid. Continue to cook, uncovered, until all the liquid has gone – this may take as long as 30 minutes. Then whizz them in the food processor with the breadcrumbs and season with salt and pepper.

450 g/1 lb button mushrooms
25 g/1 oz/2 tbsp butter
75 g/3 oz/1½ cups soft breadcrumbs
sea salt
freshly ground black pepper

parsley stuffing balls

Mix all the ingredients together, adding grated lemon rind and juice and salt and pepper to taste. Roll the mixture into balls about the size of walnuts and put them, a little apart, in a greased baking pan. Bake them for about 25 minutes in the oven preheated to 190°C/375°F/Gas 5, turning them after about 15 minutes so that they become crisp all over.

350 g/12 oz/6 cups soft white breadcrumbs
175 g/6 oz/¾ cup softened butter
1 onion, peeled and grated
2 tsp dried mixed herbs
6–8 tbsp chopped fresh parsley
grated rind of 1–2 lemons
lemon juice
sea salt
freshly ground black pepper

wild mushroom and madeira sauce

10 g/¼ oz/¼ cup dried wild mushrooms
600 ml/1 pint/2½ cups water
25 g/1 oz/2 tbsp butter
1 small onion, peeled and thinly sliced
2 tsp cornflour (cornstarch)
2 tbsp Madeira
1 tbsp soy sauce
sea salt
freshly ground black pepper

Wash the wild mushrooms to remove any grit, then put them into the water, bring to the boil and leave to soak for 30–60 minutes. Drain, keeping the liquid and chop the mushrooms.

Meanwhile, melt the butter in a saucepan, add the onion and fry for 10 minutes, letting it brown. Add the mushrooms and their soaking liquid and simmer for 30 minutes, until they are tender. Mix the cornflour (cornstarch) with the Madeira and soy sauce, add to the mushroom mixture and bring to the boil to thicken slightly. Season with salt and pepper.

leeks cooked in spiced wine

Clean and trim the leeks and cut them into 5 cm/2 inch lengths. Heat the oil in a large saucepan, add the leeks and stir-fry gently for about 5 minutes. Add the bayleaf and spices, some salt and the wine. Cover and let the leeks simmer gently for 15–20 minutes, until they are tender. Check the seasoning, then put the leeks and their liquid on to a serving dish. Sprinkle with chopped parsley and serve immediately.

700 g/1½ lb thin leeks
2 tbsp olive oil
1 bayleaf
1 tsp coriander seeds
6 peppercorns
sea salt
150 ml/5 fl oz/⅔ cup white or red wine
chopped fresh parsley

cock's comb roast potatoes

I kg/2 lb potatoes
50 g/2 oz/4 tbsp butter
sea salt

Set the oven to 190°C/375°F/Gas 5. Choose even-sized potatoes and scrub them. Put them into a saucepan, cover with water and parboil for 5 minutes or until they are reasonably tender. With a sharp knife, remove the skins and cut the potatoes in half widthways. Stand each potato on its cut surface in a roasting pan, then cut slits about 5 mm/¼ inch apart in the top.

Melt the butter, brush this all over the potatoes, then sprinkle them with salt. Bake in the oven for 45–60 minutes, or until they are golden and crisp.

carrot purée

Scrub or peel the carrots, then cut them into even-sized pieces. Put them into a saucepan, cover with water and bring to the boil. Cook, with a lid on the pan, until they are tender, about 15 minutes. Drain them, keeping the water, then mash or purée them thoroughly. Add the butter and cream, or enough of the reserved cooking water to make a soft purée. Season with salt, pepper and nutmeg.

If you're not serving this immediately, let it get cold, then reheat it over a very gentle heat, stirring often. Or put the purée into a vegetable dish, cover and bake in the oven preheated to 190°C/375°F/Gas 5 for 30 minutes, or until it's heated right through – it helps to turn the sides to the middle after about 20 minutes.

700 g/1½ lb carrots
25 g/1 oz/2 tbsp butter
150 ml/5 fl oz/⅔ cup single (light) cream – optional
sea salt
freshly ground black pepper
grated nutmeg

FOR THE REMAINDER OF THE MENU
Exotic Fruit Salad and Passion Fruit and Lime Sorbet pages 146 and 151
Mince Pies page 10

menu 4
countdown

MAKE IN ADVANCE

- Celery and Stilton Soup: make 2–4 weeks ahead, without adding the cheese, and freeze.
- Yuletide Ring and Parsley Stuffing Balls: freeze, uncooked, for 2–4 weeks.
- Wild Mushroom and Madeira Sauce: can be made in advance and frozen.
- Passion Fruit and Lime Sorbet: make up to 14 days ahead, cover and freeze.
- Mince Pies: cook a batch and freeze – it's easiest to have a batch for heating through on Christmas Day.

CHRISTMAS EVE

- Remove from the freezer: Celery and Stilton Soup, Yuletide Ring, Parsley Stuffing Balls, Wild Mushroom and Madeira Sauce, Soup; also Carrot Purée and Leeks in Spiced Wine, if you've managed to get them done.
- Put the Mince Pies on to a serving dish. Leave everything to thaw overnight.
- If you haven't done the carrots and leeks you can do so now, then cool, cover and keep in the fridge overnight. Parboil, cut and butter the potatoes as described in the recipe, and leave covered in the roasting pan. Put the stuffing balls on to a baking sheet and cover.
- Get together serving dishes – a large one for the Yuletide Ring; vegetable dishes for the potatoes, leeks and carrots; gravy boat for the sauce; a round serving dish for the fruit and sorbet. Gather plates for the first course, main course and pudding.

CHRISTMAS DAY

- ⏰ **11.30 am** Lay the table. This can be done on Christmas Eve if you're in the mood and don't need the table for breakfast. Chill the white wine.

- ⏰ **11.00 am** Set the oven to 180°C/350°F/Gas 4. Prepare the garnish for the ring.

- ⏰ **12.00 pm** Put the potatoes into the oven, towards the top. Make the Exotic Fruit Salad.

- ⏰ **12.15 pm** Put the ring into the middle of the oven.

- ⏰ **12.20 pm** Reheat the vegetables, either by stirring gently in saucepans over the heat, or in a microwave. Put them into warmed dishes, cover and put into the bottom of the oven.

- ⏰ **12.30 pm** Put the stuffing balls into the top of the oven. Open the red wine. Reheat the sauce, then serve out and keep warm in the oven – or in a baking tin of hot water, as for the vegetables.

- ⏰ **12.50 pm** Reheat the soup gently and stir in the grated cheese.

- ⏰ **12.55 pm** Open the white wine; light the candles; put the sorbet into the fridge. Serve the soup into warmed bowls and take to the table. Remove the ring from the oven and leave, covered, on one side.

- ⏰ **1.00 pm** Dinner is served.

- ⏰ **After the first course** Turn the ring out on to a warmed plate and fill the centre with stuffing balls; garnish. Quickly serve out the sauce if you haven't already done so. Serve out the potatoes. Take all the main course dishes to the table.

- ⏰ **After the main course** Sprinkle the mince pies with sugar; take to the table with the puddings.

menu 5

Two-Pear Salad

Christmas Savoury Strudel
Port Wine Sauce
Root Vegetable Purée
Buttered Broccoli • Whole Baby Carrots

Christmas Dried Fruit Salad with Cream
or Chocolate or Vanilla Ice Cream

Mince Pies

Wines: Graves or Sancerre (white)
St Emilion or Pinot Noir (red)

two-pear salad

The combination of soft, sweet comice pear and buttery avocado is very good. Both pears need to be ripe; I find it best to buy them 5–7 days in advance and let them ripen up at room temperature.

Peel and core the sweet pears, then slice them downwards into thin sections. Halve and peel the avocados and remove the stones (pits). Cut the avocados, too, into long thin slices. Sprinkle the sliced pears with the lemon juice, salt and pepper.

Put a few watercress leaves on each plate, then arrange alternate slices of comice pear and avocado on top.

2 large ripe comice pears
2 large ripe avocados
juice of $1/2$ lemon
sea salt
freshly ground black pepper
40 g/$1^1/_2$ oz/$1^1/_2$ cups watercress

christmas savoury strudel

The rich, wine-flavoured filling, the crunchy cashew nuts and the crisp, buttery pastry, are a very good combination here. Pecan or pine nuts are also delicious.

3 tbsp olive oil

2 onions, peeled and chopped

2–3 cloves garlic, peeled and crushed

2 x 400 g/14 oz cans tomatoes

1 tsp dried basil

90 ml/3 fl oz/¹/₃ cup red wine

225 g/8 oz/2 cups button mushrooms, washed and sliced

sea salt

freshly ground black pepper

275 g/10 oz filo pastry

100 g/4 oz/¹/₂ cup butter, melted

90 g/312 oz/³/₄ cup roasted cashew nuts, roughly chopped

Heat the oil in a large saucepan, add the onions and cook covered, for about 10 minutes, until tender but not browned. Add the garlic, tomatoes with their liquid, basil and wine. Simmer gently uncovered, stirring occasionally, until the liquid has disappeared and the mixture is quite thick – about 20 minutes. Add the mushrooms and cook for a further 15 minutes or so, until any liquid has boiled away. The mixture must be quite dry. Remove from the heat, season to taste and leave to cool.

When the filling is cool, you can assemble the strudel and cook it straight away, or keep it in the fridge for a few hours, or in the freezer for at least a month.

Set the oven to 200°C/400°F/Gas 6. If you have long and narrow filo – about 30 x 20 cm/ 12 x 8 inches – lay two sheets side by side on a large baking sheet, overlapping them slightly where they join. If you have pastry which is quite large – about 30 cm/12 inches or so square – lay out one sheet. Brush the surface with melted butter then sprinkle with a third of the nuts. Put another layer of filo on top, brush with butter, and scatter with nuts. Repeat with another layer, then a final layer of filo, which you just brush with butter. Tip the filling on top and spread it to about 2.5 cm/1 inch of the edges. Fold the edges over, to enclose the edge of the filling then, starting from one of the long edges, roll up like a Swiss (jelly) roll. Brush with more melted butter, and garnish with some shreds or shapes of filo. Bake for 30 minutes, or until golden brown.

root vegetable purée

Peel the vegetables and cut them into even-sized chunks.
Put them into a saucepan, cover with water and boil until
they are both tender, about 15 minutes. Drain them,
keeping the liquid, then mash them thoroughly using a
potato masher or by pushing them through a vegetable
mill. Add the butter and cream, and salt and pepper to
taste, and enough of the cooking water to make a soft,
creamy purée. Snip some parsley over the top.

225 g/8 oz celeriac (celery
root)
450 g/1 lb potatoes
25 g/1 oz/2 tbsp butter
3–4 tbsp cream
sea salt
freshly ground black pepper

to garnish:
sprigs of fresh parsley

buttered broccoli

450 g/1 lb broccoli
25 g/1 oz/2 tbsp butter
sea salt
freshly ground black pepper

Cut the thick stalks from the broccoli, then peel off the outer skin and cut the stalks into matchsticks. Separate the florets, halving any larger ones, so that they are all roughly the same size.

When you are ready to cook the broccoli – just a few minutes before you want to eat it – bring 2.5 cm/1 inch of water to the boil in a large saucepan. Add the broccoli, put a lid on the pan and cook for 3 minutes. Test the broccoli – it should be just tender when pierced with a knife. Immediately remove from the heat, drain – the water makes good stock – and put the broccoli back into the saucepan with the butter and some salt and freshly ground black pepper to taste.

whole baby carrots

These carrots are delicious cooked in a steamer over another vegetable, such as potatoes. Watch them carefully as they cook quickly if they are really tiny; the timing will depend on the size, but could be as little as 4–5 minutes for really baby ones, while bigger carrots could take up to 15 minutes.

Drain the carrots, then return to the hot saucepan or put into a warmed serving dish. Add the butter, seasoning and a squeeze of lemon juice, and mix gently to distribute the butter.

450 g/1 lb baby carrots, scrubbed
25 g/1 oz/2 tbsp butter
squeeze of lemon juice
sea salt
freshly ground black pepper

FOR THE REMAINDER OF THE MENU:

Port Wine Sauce page 109
Christmas Dried Fruit Salad page 143
Ice Creams pages 157 and 149
Mince Pies page 10

menu 5
countdown

MAKE IN ADVANCE

⏰ Christmas Savoury Strudel: freeze, uncooked, for 2–4 weeks.

⏰ Port Wine Sauce: can be made in advance and frozen.

⏰ Root Vegetable Purée: can be frozen for 2–4 weeks.

⏰ Ice Cream: make up to 14 days ahead, cover and freeze.

⏰ Mince Pies: cook a batch and freeze – it's easiest to have a batch for heating through on Christmas Day.

CHRISTMAS EVE

⏰ Remove from the freezer: Christmas Savoury Strudel, Port Wine Sauce, Root Vegetable Purée. Put the Mince Pies on to a serving dish. Leave everything to thaw overnight.

⏰ Prepare the broccoli and carrots; put them into separate plastic bags in the fridge.

⏰ Make the Christmas Dried Fruit Salad, cover and put in the fridge. If you like, put scoops of ice cream into a serving dish and refreeze, to make serving easier.

⏰ Get together serving dishes – a large one for the strudel; vegetable dishes for the purée, broccoli and carrots; a gravy boat and bowl for the sauce and cream; a round serving dish for the dried fruit salad. Gather individual plates for the first course, main course and pudding.

CHRISTMAS DAY

⏰ **11.30 am** Lay the table. This can be done on Christmas Eve if you're in the mood and don't need the table for breakfast. Chill the white wine.

⏰ **12.00 pm** Set the oven to 200°C/400°F/Gas 6. Prepare the Two-Pear Salad; cover and chill in the fridge, either in a large bowl for serving later or, if there's room in the fridge, on individual plates. Pour cream into a jug; keep in the fridge.

⏰ **12.30 pm** Put the strudel into the top of the oven. Open the red wine. Reheat the vegetable purée and the sauce, then serve out and keep warm in the oven.

⏰ **12.45 pm** Put the water on for the vegetables. Cook them until they are only just done. Drain them, put them into the warmed vegetable dishes with butter, cover with foil or lids and put them into the bottom of the oven to keep warm. Serve out the first course and take to the table.

⏰ **12.55 pm** Open the white wine; light the candles; put the ice cream into the fridge.

⏰ **1.00 pm** Dinner is served.

⏰ **After the first course** Quickly serve out the sauce if you haven't done so. Lift the strudel on to a large, warm serving dish. Put the mince pies, covered in foil, towards the bottom of the oven to warm through. Take the main course dishes to the table.

⏰ **After the main course** Sprinkle the Mince Pies with sugar; take to the table with the puddings and cream.

menu 6

Cream of Carrot Soup with Sesame Stars

Moulded Rice with Two Sauces
Favourite Stir-Fried Vegetables
Christmas Salad

Christmas Bombe

Mince Pies

Wines: Pinot Grigio or Riesling (white)
Tavel (rose) or Bardolino (red)

cream of carrot soup with sesame stars

First make the sesame stars, which can be done in advance and kept in a tin for a few days. Set the oven to 150°C/300°F/Gas 1. Sprinkle about half of the sesame seeds on to a plate. Cut the bread into stars, using a pastry cutter. Spread one side of the stars with butter, put them buttered-side down on the plate of sesame seeds, then spread butter on the other sides and sprinkle with the remaining seeds. Place on a baking sheet and bake for 1 hour, or until completely crisp and golden. Cool.

Meanwhile, make the soup. Melt the butter in a large saucepan, add the onion and fry for 5 minutes without browning. Then add the carrots and potato, cover and cook gently without browning for 10 minutes. Add the water, cover and simmer for about 20 minutes, or until the vegetables are tender.

Whizz the soup in the food processor or blender, then pass quickly through a sieve (strainer) and back into the rinsed-out saucepan. Add more water to make a nice light consistency, then add the cream, and lemon juice, salt, pepper and nutmeg to taste. Garnish with fresh herbs – dill would be particularly nice – and a swirl of cream, if you wish, and serve with the sesame stars.

25 g/1 oz/2 tbsp butter
1 onion, peeled and chopped
700 g/1½ lb carrots, sliced
225 g/8 oz/1¾ cups potato, diced
1.5 litres/2½ pints/6¼ cups water
150 ml/5 fl oz/²/₃ cup single (light) cream
squeeze of lemon juice
sea salt
freshly ground black pepper
grated nutmeg

for the sesame stars:
3–4 tbsp sesame seeds
6 slices of white or wholewheat bread
25–50 g/1–2 oz/2–4 tbsp soft butter

to garnish:
fresh herbs or extra cream

moulded rice with two sauces

This is basically a simple mixture of three types of rice. The hot cooked rice is pressed into a mould – either a large one or six individual ones – then turned out and served with red and green sauces.

1 quantity Red Pepper Sauce – opposite page
1 quantity Green Sauce – opposite page
125 g/4 oz/heaping ½ cup brown rice
50 g/2 oz/heaping ¼ cup wild rice
125 g/4 oz/heaping ½ cup white basmati rice
sea salt
freshly ground black pepper
4 spring (green) onions, finely chopped

to garnish:
fresh herbs

First make the sauces, which can be prepared well ahead and kept in the fridge until you need them.

Put the brown rice and wild rice in a sieve (strainer) and rinse under cold running water. Put into a saucepan with 450 ml/15 fl oz/2 cups water and a good pinch of salt and bring to the boil. Cover, turn the heat down very low and leave to cook for 40 minutes, when it should be tender and all the water absorbed. If not, cover and leave it to stand, off the heat, for another 15 minutes.

Meanwhile, wash the basmati rice in the same way. Put about 1.2 litres/2 pints/5 cups water into a medium-large saucepan and bring to the boil, then add the rice and a good pinch of salt. Boil, uncovered, for about 10 minutes, or until it is just tender. Drain into a sieve (strainer) and rinse with hot water. Add to the brown rice mixture, together with the onions and salt and pepper. Mix gently. Keep the rice warm over the lowest possible heat.

Have ready a 1.2 litre/2 pint/5 cup mould or six 175–200ml/6–7fl oz/¾ cup moulds – darioles or little ramekins – lightly brushed with olive oil. Spoon in the rice and press down gently, then immediately turn it out on to a warmed serving plate. Spoon the sauces in separate pools beside the rice and garnish with fresh herbs.

red pepper sauce

Halve, then quarter the red peppers, removing the stems and seeds. Place these quarters, shiny-side up, on a baking sheet or grill (broiler) pan and place under a very hot grill (broiler) until the skin is blackened and blistered. Cover the pieces with polythene or a plate, leave to get completely cold, then peel off the charred skin. Whizz the pepper in the food processor or blender, adding a little water if necessary, to make a smooth purée the consistency of double (heavy) cream. Season with salt and pepper to taste.

3 large sweet red peppers
sea salt
freshly ground black pepper

green sauce

Put the basil, pine nuts and garlic into the food processor or blender and whizz to a purée, then add the oil and lastly 8 tbsp boiling water. Season with salt and pepper to taste.

25–50 g/1–2oz/1–2 cups
fresh basil leaves
50 g/2 oz/scant $^1/_2$ cup pine nuts
1 clove garlic
8 tbsp olive oil
sea salt
freshly ground black pepper

favourite
stir-fried vegetables

4 globe artichokes

lemon juice

450 g/1 lb asparagus

225 g/8 oz shitake
mushrooms

225 g/8 oz oyster
mushrooms

3 tbsp olive oil

sea salt

freshly ground black pepper

to serve:

90 g/3½ oz/¾ cup pine
nuts, lightly toasted

First prepare the artichokes and asparagus, which can be done well in advance. Cut the leaves, stems and hairy chokes from the artichokes, leaving just the bases. Squeeze a little lemon juice over the bases to preserve the colour, then put them into a saucepan, cover with water and simmer until just tender, about 15 minutes.

While the artichokes are cooking, cut the tough stem ends off the asparagus and discard. Cut off the tips, and slice the stems slantwise into 2.5 cm/1 inch lengths. Bring 5 cm/2 inches of water to the boil in a saucepan and put in the asparagus. Boil for about 2 minutes, or until bright green and still quite crisp.

Drain both the artichokes and the asparagus into colanders and rinse under cold running water. Cut the artichoke pieces into eighths and place in a bowl. Cover with cling film until you need them.

To complete the stir-fry wash and slice the shitake mushrooms; just wash the oyster mushrooms and pat dry on kitchen paper. Heat the oil in a large saucepan or a wok if you have one, then put in the mushrooms. Cook for about 10 minutes or until the mushrooms have softened and any liquid has boiled away. Add the asparagus and artichokes and stir-fry gently for about 5 minutes or until they are heated through. Add a squeeze of lemon juice and salt and pepper to taste, sprinkle with the pine nuts and serve.

christmas salad

It is important that the cherry tomatoes are really firm, so that you can remove the skins without the tomatoes collapsing. If you can't get them, use 225 g/8 oz firm normal-size tomatoes instead, with the skin and the pulp removed, and the flesh cut into large dice. it's best to assemble this salad just before you want to serve it.

Halve, peel, stone (pit) and slice the avocado. Put the slices into a bowl and sprinkle with a little freshly squeezed lemon juice. Drain the palm hearts, cut them into 2.5 cm/1 inch slices, and add to the avocado, together with the tomatoes, basil, oil and some salt and pepper to taste. Mix gently and serve immediately.

1 large creamy ripe avocado
lemon juice
1 x 400 g/14 oz can palm hearts
225 g/8 oz cherry tomatoes, peeled
a few fresh basil leaves, roughly torn
1 tbsp olive oil
sea salt
freshly ground black pepper

FOR THE REMAINDER OF THE MENU
Christmas Bombe page 154
Mince Pies page 10

menu 6
countdown

MAKE IN ADVANCE

- Cream of Carrot Soup: freeze for 2–4 weeks.
- Sesame Stars: freeze for 2–4 weeks.
- Red Pepper Sauce: freeze for 2–4 weeks.
- Christmas Bombe: make up to 14 days ahead, cover and freeze.
- Mince Pies: cook a batch and freeze – it's easiest to have a batch for heating through on Christmas Day.

CHRISTMAS EVE

- Remove from the freezer: Cream of Carrot Soup, Sesame Stars, Red Pepper Sauce. Put the Mince Pies on to a serving dish. Leave everything to thaw overnight.
- Prepare the vegetables for the stir-fry; put them into separate plastic bags in the fridge. Toast the pine nuts. Make the rice mixture and keep in a glass or metal bowl to make it easier to reheat; cover. Cook the potatoes for the salad then cool before combining with the rest of the ingredients.
- Make the Green Sauce; put into a serving dish, cover and keep in the fridge.
- Get together serving dishes – a large one to hold the rice, either in little timbales or turned out of a large mould; jugs/bowls for the sauces; a round plate for the bombe. Gather individual plates for the first course, main course and dessert.

CHRISTMAS DAY

- **11.00 am** Lay the table. This can be done on Christmas Eve if you're in the mood and don't need the table for breakfast. Chill the white wine.

- **11.45 am** Set the bowl of rice, covered with foil, over a pan of simmering water to reheat. Prepare the garnish for the Moulded Rice.

- **12.15 pm** Make the Christmas Salad; cover and keep in a cool place.

- **12.30 pm** Open the red wine. Reheat the sauces, then serve them out and keep them warm in their pans over a very low heat. Or stand the pans in a roasting pan of steaming water over a low heat. Turn the rice into oiled small dariole moulds or one large mould. Keep warm in hot water over a hot plate or in a cool oven set to 150°C/300°F/Gas 1.

- **12.45 pm** Make the stir-fried vegetables. When they are done, turn off the heat. Put the bombe into the fridge to soften it a bit.

- **12.55 pm** Reheat the soup; put the sesame stars into a serving dish; open the white wine; light the candles.

- **1.00 pm** Dinner is served.

- **After the first course** Quickly serve out the sauces if you haven't already done so. Turn the heat on under the stir-fry and give the mixture another quick stir as it reheats, then serve out and sprinkle with the pine nuts. Turn the rice out on to a warmed serving dish. Put the mince pies, covered in foil, towards the bottom of the oven to warm through. Take the main course dishes to the table.

- **After the main course** Sprinkle the mince pies with sugar and take to the table. Turn out the bombe and take it to the table.

festive desserts

Even if you eat abstemiously most of the year I think it's good to have something a bit different once a year at Christmas. At the same time, many Christmas main courses are quite rich and filling, and for these a light dessert is required. So the recipes in this section range from the simple and refreshing, such as Christmas Dried Fruit Salad, Orange Slices with Flower Water, Exotic Fruit Salad and Figs with Rosemary Coulis, which are great to round off a substantial meal, to the luxurious and indulgent, such as Chocolate Charlotte, Christmas Bombe and Meringue Nests with Several Fillings – wonderful and wicked for those special occasions.

The dishes here can be mixed and matched with recipes in the rest of the book to make up menus suitable for various occasions over Christmas. For a balanced menu, it's best to avoid serving a fruity pudding if you're having a fruit-based first course; and to avoid having a creamy pudding if the first and/or main course contain cream, or are particularly rich. And it's probably not a wonderful idea to serve a particularly filling nut roast with a scrumptiously hearty dish like Lemon Surprise Pudding.

Some of these puddings make excellent alternatives to the traditional Christmas Pudding on Christmas Day. I've included a special Light Christmas Pudding so that you can be both traditional and modern, and a choice of two or more contrasting dishes will provide a great finale to a buffet or fork party. I'm not usually a pudding person, but sometimes for a special occasion over Christmas, I quite like having a portion of favourite pudding instead of a main meal, perhaps with some good strong black coffee – a real treat.

Most of the puddings in this chapter here either freeze well or are easy to whizz up very quickly from fresh and/or storecupboard ingredients. The accent throughout is on minimal preparation – and maximum enjoyment.

light christmas pudding

I've adapted this deliciously light, fruity pudding without any flour from Doris Grant's Christmas pudding recipe in *Food Combining For Health*. Unlike a traditional Christmas pudding, you make it just before you want to eat it (although you need to soak the prunes two days before), and steam for about three hours. Serve with Rum Sauce (page 28).

Cover the prunes with plenty of water and leave them to soak for 2 days.

Drain them, saving the water. Remove their stones (pits) and put the prunes into a food processor with half the sultanas and all but 50 g/2 oz/½ cup of the raisins. Whizz to a purée. Tip the mixture into a bowl and add the remaining sultanas and raisins, the chopped walnuts, juice of the orange and rind if you're using this, the ground almonds, brandy, egg yolks and 150 ml/5 fl oz/⅔ cup of the reserved prune water. For a spicy, traditional Christmas pudding flavour, add the mixed spice; without it, the pudding tastes rich and fruity. Mix well to a medium-soft consistency

Grease the pudding bowl(s) with butter, then spoon in the pudding mixture, leaving plenty of room at the top for it to rise. Cover with a circle of greaseproof (waxed) paper, put on a lid if the bowl has one or secure with some foil, or a pudding cloth over the top. Stand the pudding or puddings in a saucepan with boiling water to come two thirds of the way up the sides, and steam for 3 hours for the large pudding and 1½ hours for the small ones.

Loosen the edges and turn out on to a warmed serving dish or individual plates.

This pudding freezes well either cooked or uncooked – if you freeze cooked, defrost then cook for 45 minutes for large, 35 minutes for small.

makes one 1.2 litre/ 2 pint/5 cup pudding or six 175 g/6 oz ones

90 g/3½ oz/⅔ cup prunes

300 g/11 oz/heaping 2 cups sultanas

200 g/7 oz/1½ cups large raisins

75 g/3 oz/¾ cup finely chopped walnuts

juice of 1 small orange, and grated rind if untreated

125 g/4 oz/1⅓ cups ground almonds

90 ml/3 fl oz/⅓ cup brandy

2 egg yolks

1 tsp ground mixed spice – optional

snowy trifle

I don't make trifle very often, but when I do, I like to make it with home-made cake and proper, vanilla-flavoured egg custard. The result is a light, delicate, very 'snowy' and absolutely delectable dessert.

serves 6

1 Raspberry Roulade – page 167

4 tbsp sherry or sweet wine

for the custard:
600 ml/1 pint/2¹/₂ cups milk
1 vanilla pod (bean)
4 egg yolks or 1 whole egg and 2 egg yolks
40 g/1¹/₂ oz/3 tbsp caster (superfine) sugar
2 tsp cornflour (cornstarch)
300 ml/10 fl oz/1¹/₄ cups whipping cream

to serve:
50 g/2 oz/²/₃ cup flaked almonds, toasted

First, make the custard. Put the milk into a saucepan with the vanilla and bring to the boil. Remove from the heat, cover and leave to infuse for about 15 minutes.

Meanwhile, whisk together the eggs, sugar and cornflour (cornstarch), just to blend. Strain the milk on to the egg mixture, then pour the whole lot back into the saucepan and stir over a gentle heat for a few minutes until the mixture thickens – don't let it boil. It's done when it's thick enough to coat the spoon thinly. When you get to that point, take it off the heat and leave on one side for the moment. Wash and dry the vanilla pod (bean)– it can be used many times.

Cut the cake into slices, put these into a wide shallow dish, preferably glass, and sprinkle the sherry on top. Strain the custard over the top, then put it into the fridge to chill for about an hour, and to allow it to set a bit. Once this has happened, whip the cream and spread it lightly all over the top, then chill again until required. Sprinkle the toasted almonds on top just before serving.

chocolate charlotte

This amount is right for a 20 cm/8 inch loose-based tin (pan), serving 14 people – a real party piece. The holly leaves are quite difficult to make, but I find that using a good-quality chocolate – one with at least 60 per cent cocoa solids – really helps. Use very flat leaves if you can find them.

The chocolate leaves can be made in advance if you wish; they will keep in a tin, with greaseproof (waxed) paper between the layers. The leaves should be clean and completely dry. Melt the chocolate then, holding a leaf by its stem, pull it through the chocolate, until the top is covered. Make sure it is really thick. Leave it, chocolate side up, until completely cold and set overnight is best. Don't put the leaves into the fridge, or you might get white spots on them. Once they are completely set, peel the leaves away from the chocolate.

To make the charlotte, arrange sponge (lady) fingers all round the edge of the tin (pan), then sprinkle half the rum in the base and arrange more sponge (lady) fingers over the base, to cover it more or less, breaking them as necessary to fit. They don't have to be neat. Sprinkle the rest of the rum evenly on top.

Next, make the filling. Melt the chocolate and single (light) cream in a bowl set over a saucepan of simmering water. Remove from the heat and cool, then whisk hard until it's thick and light – an electric whisk is best for this.

Spoon the chocolate mixture into the tin (pan). Chill in the fridge until firm.

To serve, remove the charlotte from the tin (pan) to a serving dish. Decorate with the cream whipped with the rum, holly leaves and a dusting of grated chocolate.

serves 14

for the holly leaves:
125 g/4 oz/²/₃ cup plain (bitter sweet) chocolate, chopped
10 or more holly leaves, not too hard or curvy

for the charlotte:
2 x 200 g/7 oz packets sponge (lady) fingers
6 tbsp rum
450 g/1 lb/2²/₃ cups plain chocolate, chopped
600 ml/1 pint/2¹/₂ cups single (light) cream

to decorate:
150 ml/5 fl oz/²/₃ cup whipping cream
1 tbsp rum
grated chocolate
a festive ribbon – optional

orange slices
with flower water

This deliciously refreshing fruit salad is best made ahead of serving to allow the flavours to mellow – it can be made a day or two in advance and kept well covered in the fridge. Remove from the fridge for an hour or so before serving. Serve with Vegan Cream (page 25) for a luxurious yet light dessert.

serves 6

9 oranges
honey – Greek, or orange
flower if possible
a few drops of orange
flower water

Scrub one of the oranges thoroughly. Set aside. With a zester, pare off the outer coloured zest in long, thin delicate shreds.

Holding the oranges over a bowl, use a sharp, serrated stainless steel knife to cut away the peel and pith together, round and round, like peeling an apple in one go. Slice the orange flesh into thin circles or sections between the membranes. Add the zest. Sweeten to taste with a little honey and add the orange flower water. Cover and leave until ready to serve.

christmas dried fruit salad

This is very easy to make and good to eat – it's lovely with thick Greek yogurt. Add a tablespoon of orange flower water to this dried fruit salad to give it extra fragrance.

Wash the dried fruit, then put it into a bowl, cover with plenty of water and leave to soak overnight.

Next day, put the fruit into a saucepan with its soaking water and more, if necessary, to make it just level with the top of the fruit. Add the sugar and cinnamon stick and bring to the boil. Let the mixture simmer away, without a lid on the pan, for about an hour, or until nearly all the liquid has boiled away.

Remove from the heat and add the rum and nuts. Leave to cool, then serve at room temperature.

serves 4–6

450 g/1 lb mixed dried fruit – peaches, apricots, prunes, pears, apples, figs, raisins
50 g/2 oz/$^1/_4$ cup soft brown or demerara sugar
1 cinnamon stick, broken in half
6 tbsp rum or brandy
90 g/3$^1/_2$ oz/$^2/_3$ cup blanched almonds

figs with raspberry coulis

An out-of-season treat ... if you can get fresh ripe figs at Christmas, and have some
Raspberry Coulis (page 27) in the freezer, this dessert is light, easy and delicious.

You need 1 fresh fig for each person, 2–3 tablespoons of raspberry coulis and, if you
like, a good heaped dessertspoonful of thick Greek yogurt. Wash the figs and pat them
dry on kitchen paper. Cut them downwards, through the stem but not completely through
the base, making three cuts, so that you end up with six segments still attached to the
base. Serve with a little pool of coulis, and yogurt if you're using this.

meringue nests

These small meringues have 3 different fillings, so each person can have one of each.

To make the orange liqueur filling, beat the cream until thick, then stir in the orange rind and liqueur. Pile into four meringue nests and decorate with glacé (candied) fruits and chopped angelica.

To make the fruit filling, chop your selection of fresh fruit and whip the cream until thick; divide between four nests.

To make the ginger filling, beat the cream until thick, then stir in two-thirds of the ginger. Spoon into the remaining nests and use the rest of the ginger and the chocolate to decorate the tops.

serves 4

12 Meringue Nests – page 26

orange liqueur filling:
150 ml/5 fl oz/²/₃ cup whipping cream
1 tsp grated orange rind
2 tbsp orange liqueur

fruit filling:
fresh fruit, such as strawberries, kiwi, grapes
150 ml/5 fl oz/²/₃ cup whipping cream

ginger filling:
150 ml/5 fl oz/²/₃ cup whipping cream
25 g/1 oz/2 tbsp chopped preserved ginger

to decorate:
red and yellow glacé fruits
chopped angelica
chocolate curls
grated chocolate

exotic fruit salad

This is one of the simplest, prettiest and most refreshing desserts, and makes a lovely contrast to some of the richer and more filling Christmas and winter dishes. Choose your own selection of fruits, aiming for plenty of different colours and textures. I think they look best arranged on a round glass plate, and they are delicious eaten on their own, or with thick Greek yogurt or sorbet.

serves 6

6 lychees
I ripe papaya (paw-paw) or
2 pomegranates
1 nectarine
2 figs
12 cape gooseberries
(physalis)
225 g/8 oz/heaping ¹/₂ cup
strawberries
125 g/4 oz/1 cup
raspberries, golden or red
1 star fruit (carambola)

to decorate:
a few sprigs of fresh mint

Using a stainless knife which won't give the fruit a metallic flavour, peel the lychees and papaya (paw-paw), and remove the stones (pits) and seeds. Remove the stone (pit) from the nectarine. Cut the flesh into neat pieces, not too small. If you are using pomegranates, halve them then, holding each half over a bowl to catch the delicious crimson juice, ease out the seeds with a small pointed teaspoon (a grapefruit spoon is ideal), or the point of a knife. Discard the skin. Slice the figs into thin circles. Pull back the petals on the cape gooseberries (physalis). Wash the strawberries and raspberries. Wash, then thinly slice the star fruit (carambola). Arrange each type of fruit in a pile on a large platter, then decorate with a few sprigs of fresh mint.

lemon and ginger cheesecake

I call this cheesecake, but really it's a bit of a cheat one, because it doesn't contain cheese – just a beautifully smooth, lemony cream which sets like a cheesecake, on a crisp ginger base. It's easy to make and an unfailingly popular party dessert. It's rich, so a little goes a long way. To crush the biscuits (cookies), put them in a plastic bag and crush to coarse crumbs with a rolling pin.

Melt the butter in a medium saucepan, then stir in the crumbs and ground ginger. Press this mixture into the base of an 18–20 cm/7–8 inch springform cake pan – the base of a jam jar is useful for pressing the crumbs firmly into the pan. Put into the fridge to chill.

Now make the filling: whisk the cream until it is almost fully whipped, then add the condensed milk and whisk again, until very thick. Finally, stir in the lemon rind and juice. The mixture may look as if it's going to separate at first, but don't worry, it won't; just keep on stirring gently until it is very smooth and thick.

Spoon this mixture on top of the ginger base, then smooth and level it with the back of a spoon or a spatula. Cover and chill for several hours, then remove the outside of the springform pan and decorate the top of the cheesecake with lemon peel and ginger before serving.

This cheesecake can be made at least 24 hours in advance; it keeps very well for several days in the fridge, but keep it tightly covered so that it doesn't absorb any other flavours.

serves 8–12

75 g/3 oz/6 tbsp butter
200 g/7 oz/scant 2 cups ginger biscuits (cookies), crushed
$^1/_2$ tsp ground ginger
300 ml/10 fl oz/1$^1/_4$ cups double (heavy) cream
218g/8 oz can condensed milk
grated rind and juice of 1 lemon

to decorate:
candied lemon peel
chopped preserved ginger

rum-macerated fruits with coconut and lime cream

serves 6

1 ripe pineapple

2 bananas

1 ripe papaya (paw-paw)

grated rind and juice of 1 lime

50 g/2 oz/¹⁄₄ cup brown sugar

4 tbsp dark rum

125 g/4 oz/²⁄₃ cup creamed coconut, chopped

extra sugar or honey to taste

Cut the skin from the pineapple, making sure you've taken out all the little black bits, then remove the central core and cut the flesh into dice. Peel the bananas and slice into chunks. Peel, deseed and slice the papaya (paw-paw) and add to the pineapple with half the lime juice, the sugar and rum. Cover and leave the mixture to macerate for at least 1 hour, stirring gently from time to time.

Meanwhile, make the cream. Put the coconut into a small saucepan with 300 ml/10 fl oz/1¹⁄₄ cups boiling water. Stir until dissolved, heating gently if necessary. Remove from the heat and leave until completely cold.

Stir in the lime rind and remaining juice, and a little sugar or honey to taste. It will thicken as it gets cold, especially if you chill it in the fridge. Serve with the fruit.

vanilla ice cream

I've made many vanilla ice creams over the years, some with a light egg custard base, delicately flavoured with vanilla; others using the meringue method, with a sugar syrup poured on to eggs … the one my family always ask for is the simplest of them all: just whipping cream and condensed milk.

All you do is whip the cream until it's almost fully whipped, then whisk in the condensed milk and 2 tsp vanilla extract. Pour the mixture into a suitable container and freeze, without a lid, until solid. The proportions I use are 600 ml/1 pint/2½ cups whipping cream to a 405 g/14 oz can skimmed condensed milk. This makes a lot, but it keeps very well in the freezer.

For a simple but luxurious dessert, I love this ice cream served with Raspberry Coulis (page 27), which gives just the right touch of sharpness, and some baby macaroons or ratafias.

You can add other flavourings to the basic ice cream: a coffee version is particularly good, as the coffee cuts the sweetness of the condensed milk. For this I use a good-quality instant coffee – 1–2 tablespoons – dissolved in a little boiling water and added with the condensed milk.

lemon curd ice cream

This tangy, refreshing ice cream can be made in moments. If you have some home-made lemon curd, this is a delicious way to use it; otherwise buy the best-quality pale-coloured lemon curd, or lemon cheese, that you can find. This ice cream is good served with Raspberry Coulis (page 27).

serves 6

312g/10 oz jar lemon curd
600 ml/1 pint/2½ cups natural low-fat yogurt
300 ml/10 fl oz/1¼ cups whipping cream

Put the lemon curd into a bowl and mix until smooth, then gradually beat in the yogurt then the cream, to make a smooth, creamy mixture. Pour this into a rigid freezerproof container and freeze until firm. The ice cream sets very hard, so you need to remove it from the freezer in good time – let it stand at room temperature for 30–45 minutes, or in the fridge for at least an hour before you want to serve it.

passion fruit and lime sorbet

This sorbet is easy to make and has a wonderful flavour. I like it with the passion fruit seeds left in, because they give a good crunchy texture and pretty speckled appearance; however most people, including my own family, prefer it without them.

Dissolve the sugar in the water over a low heat, then bring to the boil and boil for 3–4 minutes to make a sugar syrup. Remove from the heat and set aside to cool.

Scoop all the pulp and seeds out of the passion fruits, pass them through a nylon sieve (strainer) to remove the seeds if you wish and add the purée to the cooled sugar syrup. Wash the lime, then remove long thin shreds of coloured zest; put these into a plastic bag and keep until needed.

Squeeze the lime and add the juice to the passion fruit mixture. Transfer the mixture to a rigid freezerproof container and freeze, uncovered, until solid – about 6 hours, or overnight.

Cut the mixture into small chunks and put these into the food processor. Whizz for a minute or two until the sorbet is soft and fluffy, then put back into the container and freeze again.

When the mixture is frozen but not too hard, put small scoops of it on to a plate and refreeze. This makes the sorbet easier to serve. Decorate with the lime rind just before serving.

serves 6

350 g/12 oz/1¾ cups
caster (superfine) sugar
600 ml/1 pint/2½ cups
water
12 passion fruits
1 lime

lemon surprise pudding

This is an easy-to-make, popular family pudding, and another one which contrasts pleasantly with spicy Christmas foods. The mixture separates as it cooks, resulting in a light lemon sponge on top of a sharp, citrus sauce.

serves 4–6

125 g/4 oz/¹/₂ cup butter
125 g/4 oz/heaping ¹/₂ cup caster (superfine) sugar
125 g/4 oz/2/4 cup + 2 tbsp self-raising flour
grated rind of 1 lemon
2 eggs
a little milk

for the sauce:
75 g/3 oz/scant ¹/₂ cup caster (superfine) sugar
2 tbsp cornflour (cornstarch)
juice of 1 lemon

Set the oven to 190°C/375°F/Gas 5.

Make the sponge mixture by creaming together the butter, sugar, flour, lemon rind and eggs. Beat well for about 2 minutes, until smooth and glossy, adding a little milk or water – about 2 tablespoons – if necessary for a soft consistency. Spoon the mixture into a lightly greased shallow baking dish; it should only half fill it.

Now make the sauce. Put the sugar and cornflour (cornstarch) into a bowl with the lemon juice and mix together, then gradually add 300 ml/10 fl oz/1¹/₂ cups boiling water, stirring all the time. Pour this sauce over the sponge mixture in the dish, then bake for about 40–45 minutes, or until the mixture has risen and feels firm to the touch. Serve hot or warm.

cinnamon torte

I like lemon curd or apricot jam instead of raspberry jam sometimes in this torte.

Sift the flour and cinnamon into a bowl or food processor, then put in the ground almonds, sugar, butter and grated lemon rind. Process, without the plunger to let in more air and make the mixture light, or rub the fat into the other ingredients with your fingers. Either way, the result will be a soft dough. You can roll this out straight away, but it's easier to handle if you wrap it and chill it for 30 minutes.

Set the oven to 180°C/350°F/Gas 4. On a lightly floured board, roll out two-thirds of the almond mixture, to fit a 20 cm/8 inch quiche pan or dish pan. Put the pastry into the tin and trim the edges. Spread the jam over the pastry, then roll out the remaining pastry, including the trimmings, and cut long strips to make a lattice across the top of the jam. Bake the torte for 30 minutes, or until the pastry is set and lightly browned. Serve hot or cold, with a snowy topping of sifted icing (confectioners') sugar.

125 g/4 oz/^{3}/$_4$ cup + 2 tbsp
self-raising flour
1 tsp ground cinnamon
125 g/4 oz/1^1/$_3$ **cups ground**
almonds
125 g/4 oz/heaping ^{1}/$_2$ **cup**
caster (superfine) sugar
125 g/4 oz/^{1}/$_2$ **cup butter**
grated rind of 1 lemon
225 g/8 oz/^{3}/$_4$ **cup raspberry**
jam

to serve:
icing (confectioners') sugar

christmas bombe

When you cut this snowy white ice cream bombe, a golden inner layer flecked with brightly-coloured fruits is revealed. It's wonderful as an alternative Christmas pudding, or for a party, and it's easy to make. You need to allow plenty of time for the freezing – it's better to start making it the day before you need it, or it can be made up to four weeks in advance and stored in the freezer. It looks good with extra Cointreau-soaked fruits on top, but this makes the pudding quite boozy, so drivers should be warned.

serves 8

for the white layer:
4 egg whites
225 g/6 oz caster sugar
150 ml/5 fl oz water
450 ml/15 fl oz whipping cream
a few drops of vanilla essence

for the golden layer:
225 g/8 oz crystallized fruits, in a variety of colours
2 tbs Cointreau or other orange liqueur
4 egg yolks
4 tangerines or satsumas
100 g/4 oz caster (superfine) sugar
150 ml/5 fl oz whipping cream
extra glacé fruit, to decorate

First turn your freezer to its coldest setting and chill a 1.7 litre/3 pint/2 quart ice cream bombe mould or pudding bowl, preferably metal.

Now for the white ice cream. Put the egg whites into a bowl and whisk them until they are very stiff, as if you were making meringues. Put the sugar into a saucepan with 1150 ml/5 fl oz water. Heat gently until the sugar has dissolved, then bring to the boil and boil hard for 3 minutes. Take off the heat and immediately pour this mixture on to the egg whites, whisking them at the same time. An electric whisk makes this operation easier. Next, whip the cream until it will stand in soft peaks, then whisk it into the egg white mixture, together with a few drops of vanilla extract. Pour the whole lot into the bombe mould or bowl and freeze until firm – this may take 5–6 hours. Meanwhile, prepare the fruits for the golden layer. Cut them into 1 cm/½ inch chunks, put them into a shallow container and sprinkle with the Cointreau.

Now make the tangerine ice cream for the golden layer. Put the egg yolks into a bowl with the grated rind of two of the tangerines and whisk until pale and beginning to thicken. Squeeze the juice from all the tangerines and put this into a saucepan with the sugar. Heat gently until the sugar has dissolved, then boil hard for 3 minutes. Immediately pour this mixture over the egg yolks, whisking at the same time. When it has all been added, continue to whisk the mixture for about 5 minutes until it is very thick and light. Whip the cream to the soft peak stage, then whisk this into the tangerine mixture. Put it into the freezer and freeze for 2–3 hours, or until it is beginning to solidify but is still soft enough to stir. Add the fruits and orange liqueur to the tangerine ice cream, together with any liquid that's left over.

Hollow out the inside of the white ice cream to make a cavity for the tangerine ice. Push the bits of ice cream that you scoop out of the centre up the sides of the bombe, aiming for a thickness of about 1 cm/½ inch, although this will depend on the exact shape of your mould or bowl. Spoon the tangerine mixture into the middle and finish by smoothing any remaining white ice cream on top. Put the bombe back in the freezer and freeze for several hours until the layers are completely firm.

Unmould the bombe by dipping the mould into a bowl of hot water for a few seconds, then loosening the edges with a palette knife (metal spatula) and turning the ice cream out on to a plate. Smooth the top, then put the bombe back into the freezer until required decorated with a few pieces of glacé (candied) fruit on top. It can be served straight from the freezer as it soon softens.

boozy vegan ice cream

This simple vegan chocolate ice cream has always been a favourite with my daughters. Here it's dressed up for Christmas with the addition of some dried fruits, nuts and booze. It also makes a good frozen Christmas pudding if you freeze it in a plastic bowl.

serves 6–8

1 tbsp cornflour (cornstarch)
900 ml/1½ pints/3¾ cups soya milk
1 vanilla pod (bean)
2 tbsp sugar
50 g/2 oz/4 tbsp vegan margarine
125 g/4 oz chocolate, chopped
125 g/4 oz/scant ¾ cup glacé (candied) cherries
50 g/2 oz/⅓ cup whole mixed peel, chopped
50 g/2 oz/scant ½ cup raisins or sultanas (golden raisins)
4 tbsp rum or brandy
25 g/1 oz/⅓ cup flaked almonds

Put the cornflour (cornstarch) into a bowl and blend to a paste with a little of the milk. Put the rest of the milk into a saucepan with the vanilla, sugar, margarine and the chocolate. Heat gently to boiling point, then pour over the paste and mix until combined.

Return the mixture to the saucepan and bring to the boil, stirring. Remove from the heat, cover and leave until cool. Remove the vanilla and wash and dry it – it can be used many times, liquidize the mixture. Pour it into a container and freeze until it is solid around the edges. Whisk and return to the freezer. Repeat this process, this time whisking in the fruits, rum or brandy and almonds, then and let the ice cream freeze until solid.

Make sure this ice cream is well-softened before you use it, as it freezes very hard – an hour at room temperature is not too long. Then beat it before serving, or simply turn it out of a pudding bowl, like a Christmas pudding.

chocolate ice cream

Whisk the egg whites until they are stiff, as if you were
making meringues. Next, put the sugar and 8 tbsp water
into a small saucepan and heat gently until the sugar has
dissolved. Raise the heat and let the mixture boil for 2
minutes. Remove from the heat, and pour this over the egg
whites, whisking at the same time.

Melt the chocolate in a bowl set over a pan of
simmering water, or in the microwave, and add carefully
and gradually to the egg white mixture. Whip the cream
until it is standing in soft peaks, then fold quickly into the
mixture.

Turn the ice cream into a rigid freezerproof container
and freeze until firm.

To serve, remove from the freezer 10–15 minutes
before you need it, to soften it a little, and scoop into
sundae glasses.

Decorate with extra chocolate. White chocolate makes
a nice contrast, shaved into curls on a potato peeler. Serve
with Macaroons (page 179) if you like.

serves 6

2 egg whites
150 g/5 oz/²/₃ cup caster
(superfine) sugar
125 g/4 oz dark chocolate,
broken up
300 ml/10 fl oz/1¹/₄ cups
whipping cream
extra dark or white
chocolate, to decorate

christmas baking

Even though you can buy excellent cakes (cookies) and biscuits, there's nothing quite like the ones you've baked yourself, and I know that Christmas is a time when even people who rarely bake during the year, do so. They want simple, reliable recipes that don't take too long to make and, as with all Christmas cookery, are festive and special. I hope you will agree that the recipes in this section more than meet these requirements.

The recipes here have been chosen to contrast with, and complement, the Traditional Christmas Cake, which you will find on page 3, along with the other recipes that you can make ahead of the festive season. Don't worry if you haven't managed to prepare your festive baking in advance, though – in this section you will find a lovely Last-Minute Christmas Cake which is easy to make and wonderfully moist and delicious, as well as various 'alternative' Christmas cakes, such as Madeira Cake and Vegan Chocolate Sponge Cake; these latter ones are particularly popular with my family and, indeed, preferred by my daughters to a more traditional fruit cake. They also love a simple yeast cake at Christmas, hence the inclusion of Swedish Ring Cake, which is as easy to make as a normal cake. Some of the offerings – particularly Bûche de Noël and Light Ginger Cake with Lemon Icing – double beautifully as desserts, and are good for parties since they're easier to eat casually than more liquid desserts. The Brandy Snaps and Jean's Biscuits make excellent accompaniments to ice creams, sorbets and creamy puddings.

little christmas buns

This is another recipe with children in mind. They want something special and partyish but often dislike the rich, spicy flavours of Christmas cake and mince pies, and these little buns are always popular. You can let your imagination go when you decorate them – or if you've got the time, let the children have the fun of doing it themselves. I think the buns are pretty decorated with marzipan shapes such as crackers or holly leaves and berries, or stars cut out of fondant icing and adorned with silver balls, but children really prefer using – and eating – sweets (candies) and bits of chocolate flake.

Set the oven to 190°C/375°F/Gas 5.

Sift the flour into a bowl, then add the butter, sugar and eggs. Beat well with a wooden spoon or an electric mixer until the mixture is thick and slightly glossy-looking. Put heaped teaspoonfuls of the mixture into paper cases, which can be put into deep bun tins (muffin or cup cake pans) with a flat base, or on to a baking sheet. Bake for 15–20 minutes, until the cakes have risen and spring back to a light touch. Set aside to cool on a wire rack.

To decorate, make some glacé icing by mixing the icing (confectioners') sugar with about a tablespoonful of water; spread a little of this on top of each bun, then decorate as desired.

makes 15

175 g/6 oz/1¼ cups self-raising wholewheat flour or a half-and-half mix of white and wholewheat self-raising flour
125 g/4 oz/½ cup soft butter
125 g/4 oz/heaping ½ cup caster (superfine) sugar
2 eggs
paper cake cases
sweets (candies), marzipan shapes, etc, to decorate

for the glacé icing:
125 g/4 oz/scant 1 cup icing (confectioners') sugar

last-minute christmas cake

If you can't find small cake tins, make the little cakes by cutting the big square one into quarters then carefully sculpting into rounds.

makes one 20 cm/ 8 inch square cake or four individual 10 cm/4 inch round cakes

1 kg/2¼ lb/7¼ cups mixed dried fruit

grated rind and juice of 1 lemon

1 tbsp black treacle (molasses)

150 ml/5 fl oz/⅔ cup port

250 g/9 oz/1½ cups + 2 tbsp plain white (all-purpose) flour

1 tsp ground mixed spice

1 tsp ground cinnamon

225 g/8 oz/1 cup butter

225 g/8 oz/heaping 1 cup dark brown sugar

4 eggs

175 g/6 oz/1 cup glacé (candied) cherries

25 g/1 oz/⅓ cup flaked almonds

Put all of the dried fruit into a saucepan with the lemon rind and juice, treacle and port and bring to the boil. Remove from the heat, cover and leave to get cold. This process can be speeded up if you stand the pan in a bowl of cold water.

Meanwhile, set the oven to 150°C/300°F/Gas 2 and line a 20 cm/8 inch square or four 10 cm/ 4 inch round cake tins (pans) with greaseproof (waxed) paper.

Sift the flours with the spices on to a plate. Cream the butter and sugar until very light, then alternately beat in the fruit, eggs and flour. Finally, stir in the cherries and almonds. Spoon the mixture into the tin (pan) or tins, hollowing out the middle very slightly so that the surface will be flat. Bake the large cake for 2–3 hours and the small ones for 1½–1¾ hours, or until a skewer inserted in the middle comes out clean. It took 2½ hours to cook the large one, 1½ hours for the small ones in my oven. Leave to cool in the tin (pan).

TO PUT A NUTTY TOPPING ON THE SQUARE CAKE

This is a very quick, easy and effective topping for a Christmas cake, especially nice if you aren't too keen on almond paste and icing. The nuts should be put on the cake before it's baked.

Hollow out the middle of the cake slightly so that it will be flat when it's cooked, then arrange the nuts attractively in diagonal rows on top; be careful not to press them into the mixture or they may sink and disappear as it bakes. For a 20 cm/8 inch cake with a separate row of each one, you will need about 50 g/2 oz/½ cup blanched almonds, Brazil nuts, skinned hazelnuts, pecan nuts or walnuts. Glacé (candied) cherries would make an attractive middle row. Finish with a flourish by tying a bow of red ribbon around the sides.

TO DECORATE THE LITTLE ROUND CAKES

Cover the cakes with almond paste – page 14. Make 1 quantity of Fondant Icing and use it to decorate the cakes – page 6.

I decorate the top of one cake with marzipan fruits. Another cake I decorate with a mixture of glacé (candied) cherries, strips of angelica and crystallized orange segments, and a third with a candle and some holly. For the fourth cake, I reroll the fondant icing trimmings and cut into star shapes, using a pastry cutter, then use them to decorate the sides and top, dusting the top one with a little fine brown sugar. A final flourish is achieved by pinning festive ribbon round the sides.

vegan chocolate sponge cake

**makes one 18 cm/
7 inch cake**

175 g/6 oz/1¼ cups self-
raising flour
175 g/6 oz/scant 1 cup
caster (superfine) sugar
¾ tsp bicarbonate of soda
(baking soda)
40 g/1½ oz/⅓ cup cocoa
powder
5 tbsp soya flour
juice of 1½ lemons
150 ml/5 fl oz/⅔ cup
groundnut oil
1 tsp vanilla extract

for the buttercream:
125 g/4 oz/½ cup vegan
margarine
200 g/7 oz/scant 1½ cups
icing (confectioners') sugar
2 tbsp cocoa powder

to decorate:
a little plain vegan
chocolate

Set the oven to 180°C/350°F/Gas 4. Grease two 18 cm/ 7 inch round cake tins (pans), lining each with greased non-stick or greaseproof (waxed) paper.

Sift all the dry ingredients – the flour, sugar, soda, cocoa powder and soya flour into a large bowl. Put the lemon juice into a measuring jug and make it up to 350 ml/12 fl oz/1½ cups with cold water; mix with the oil and vanilla. Pour all this liquid into the dry ingredients and quickly mix with a wooden spoon to a smooth batter.

Pour the batter into the two tins (pans) and bake for about 35 minutes, or until the cakes spring back to a light touch. Cool them on a wire rack, then sandwich them and ice the top with a buttercream made by beating together the margarine, sugar, cocoa and enough hot water to make a light, fluffy consistency. Decorate with some shavings of plain vegan chocolate, if you wish.

madeira cake

This is another favourite cake which my daughters always ask for at Christmas. I like to use half wholewheat flour and half white, so either the plain (all-purpose) flour or the self-raising could be wholewheat.

Set the oven to 180°C/350°F/Gas 4. Grease and line a 20 cm/8 inch round cake tin (pan) with greased greaseproof (waxed) paper.

Sift the flours together on to a plate, adding any bran left in the sieve (strainer). Leave this on one side while you cream together the butter and sugar until they're light and pale – you can use an electric whisk for this then whisk in the beaten eggs, about a tablespoonful at a time, and the vanilla extract, if you're using this. Put the flour on top and fold this in very gently with a metal spoon, to keep as much air in the mixture as possible. Add a spoonful or two of milk if necessary to make a soft, dropping consistency, and spoon the mixture into the prepared pan.

Bake for 20 minutes, then carefully lay the peel on top of the cake and bake for a further 40 minutes, or until a warmed skewer inserted into the middle comes out clean. Turn out on to a wire rack to cool.

makes one 20 cm/ 8 inch cake

175 g/6 oz/1$\frac{1}{4}$ cups plain flour

175 g/6 oz/1$\frac{1}{4}$ cups self-raising flour

250 g/9 oz/1 cup + 2 tbsp butter

250 g/9 oz/1$\frac{1}{3}$ cups vanilla sugar, or caster (superfine) sugar with 1$\frac{1}{2}$ tsp vanilla extract

4 large eggs, beaten

2–3 tbsp milk – optional

2–3 thin slices of candied citron peel

drenched lemon cake

**makes one 900 g/
2 lb cake**

175 g/6 oz/1¼ cups self-
raising flour
1 tsp baking powder
175 g/6 oz/scant 1 cup
caster (superfine) sugar
125 g/4 oz/½ cup soft
butter
grated rind of 1 lemon
2 eggs
2–4 tbsp milk

for the syrup:
juice of 1 lemon
125 g/4 oz/heaping ½ cup
caster (superfine) sugar

Set the oven to 180°C/350°F/Gas 4. Prepare a 900 g/2 lb loaf tin (pan) measuring about 25 x 13 cm/10 x 5 inches. Put a long strip of non-stick paper in the pan to cover the base and come up the two narrow sides. Grease the uncovered sides of the tin (pan).

Sift the flour and baking powder into a bowl, add the sugar, butter and lemon rind, crack in the eggs. Beat vigorously with a wooden spoon or with an electric whisk until the mixture is thick, smooth and slightly glossy-looking – about 2 minutes by hand. Add a little milk to make a soft dropping consistency and mix again, then turn the mixture into the prepared tin (pan).

Bake for 40 minutes, or until the cake springs back to a light touch.

While the cake is cooking, make the syrup by mixing together the lemon juice and sugar. As soon as you take the cake out of the oven, pour the syrup evenly over the top, then leave it to get completely cold. Finally, remove the cake from the tin (pan) and strip off the paper.

light ginger cake with lemon icing

I think this light ginger cake, with its tangy lemon icing, is nicer at Christmas than the more usual dark gingerbread because it's so different from Christmas cake. It's very quick to make.

Set the oven to 170°C/325°F/Gas 3. Prepare a 450 g/1 lb loaf tin (pan) measuring about 18 x 10 x 7.5 cm/6 x 4 x 3 inches. Put a long strip of non-stick paper in the pan to cover the base and come up the two narrow sides. Grease the uncovered sides of the tin (pan) with butter.

Sift the flour, baking powder and ginger into a food processor, mixer or bowl, then put in the sugar, butter and eggs. Whizz, whisk or beat everything together until it is light, thick and slightly glossy looking. This will take about 3 minutes by hand, less time in a processor or with an electric whisk or mixer. Stir in the chopped ginger.

Spoon the mixture into the tin (pan) and gently level the top with the back of a spoon. Bake for 1 hour to 1 hour 10 minutes, or until the cake is risen, has shrunk a little from the sides of the pan, and the middle springs back to a light touch. Cool for a few minutes, then turn out on to a wire rack to finish cooling.

Finish the cake. Scrub the lemon thoroughly. With a zester, pare off the outer coloured zest in long, thin delicate shreds. Set aside, halve the lemon and squeeze the juice. To make the icing, sift the sugar into a bowl, then gradually mix in enough of the lemon juice to make a stiff mixture – you should need 1–2 tbsp. Put this on top of the cake, spreading it gently to the edges, then scatter the lemon zest over the top.

makes one 450 g/ 1 lb cake

125 g/4 oz/³/₄ cup + 2 tbsp **self-raising wholewheat flour or a half-and-half mix of white and wholewheat self-raising flour**
1 tsp baking powder
2 tsp ground ginger
125 g/4 oz/heaping ¹/₂ cup **caster (superfine) sugar**
125 g/4 oz/¹/₂ cup soft **butter**
2 eggs
50–125 g/2–4 oz/¹/₃–²/₃ cup **preserved stem ginger, roughly chopped**

for the lemon icing:
125 g/4 oz/scant 1 cup **icing (confectioners') sugar**
1 lemon

parkin

This parkin is a favourite recipe which has appeared before, but I wanted to include it as it's a useful cake for Christmas, contrasting well with other flavours and storing well – it can be made at least a week in advance and just goes on improving.

makes 12–16 pieces

125 g/4 oz/³/₄ cup + 2 tbsp plain wholewheat flour or a half-and-half mix of plain white (all-purpose) flour and wholewheat flour

2 tsp baking powder

2 tsp ground ginger

125 g/4 oz/²/₃ cup medium oatmeal

3 rounded tbsp real barbados sugar

125 g/4 oz/¹/₃ cup black treacle (molasses)

125 g/4 oz/¹/₃ cup golden syrup or honey

125 g/4 oz/¹/₂ cup butter

175 ml/6 fl oz/scant ³/₄ cup milk

optional extras:
50 g/2 oz/¹/₃ cup preserved ginger, chopped
50 g/2 oz/¹/₃ cup whole candied peel, chopped

Set the oven to 180°C/350°F/Gas 4. Line a 20 cm/8 inch square cake tin (pan) with greased greaseproof (waxed) paper.

Sift the flour, baking powder and ground ginger into a bowl, adding the residue of bran from the sieve (strainer), as well, and also the oatmeal. Put the sugar, treacle (molasses), golden syrup or honey and butter into a saucepan and heat gently until melted. Let the mixture cool until tepid, then add the milk to it. Pour the whole lot into the dry ingredients, and add the preserved ginger and candied peel if you're using these. Mix well, then pour into the prepared tin (pan).

Bake for 50–60 minutes, or until the parkin is firm to the touch. Lift the parkin out of the tin (pan), on its paper, and put it on a wire rack to cool. When it's cool, cut the parkin into pieces and remove the paper.

raspberry roulade

This is a very light cake and it's very quick and easy to make if you have an electric whisk.

The classic way to make a whisked sponge like this is to whisk the eggs and sugar over a pan of steaming water. However, if you heat the sugar for a few minutes in the oven and then add this to the eggs, you can do away with the pan of water. So, first set the oven to 200°C/400°F/Gas 6 and line a greased 23 x 32 cm/9 x 13 inch Swiss roll tin (jelly roll pan) with greased greaseproof (waxed) or non-stick paper. Even non-stick paper needs to be greased for this recipe.

Put the sugar on to a baking sheet and pop into the oven for 4–5 minutes to heat up. Break the eggs into a bowl or the bowl of an electric mixer, then tip in the sugar. Whisk for about 5 minutes, or until the mixture is very pale, light and fluffy, and the mixture will hold the impression of the whisk for several seconds. Then sift the flour and cornflour (cornstarch) in on top, and fold them in carefully with a metal spoon or thin plastic spatula.

Pour the mixture into the prepared tin (pan) and bake for 7–8 minutes – it's done when the middle springs back to a light touch. While it's cooking, lay a piece of greaseproof (waxed) paper or non-stick paper out on the work surface and dust it with cornflour (cornstarch), then turn the cake straight out on to this. Trim the short edges with a sharp knife.

Warm the jam gently in a saucepan, then pour and spread this all over the cake and quickly roll it up from one of the long sides. Brush off any excess cornflour (cornstarch), and dust with a little icing (confectioners') sugar.

makes one roll

125 g/4 oz/heaping ½ cup caster sugar
4 eggs
50 g/2 oz/6 tbsp self-raising flour
1 tbsp cornflour (cornstarch), plus extra for dusting
225 g/8 oz/heaping ⅔ cup raspberry jam

to decorate:
a little icing (confectioners') sugar

bûche de noël

Bûche de Noël is French for Christmas log – it is the traditional Christmas cake in France, where it is often made with chestnuts. This is my version using chocolate.

serves 6–8

4 eggs
175 g/6 oz/scant 1 cup caster (superfine) sugar
50 g/2 oz/¹/₂ cup cocoa powder
2 egg whites

for the special buttercream:
125 g/4 oz/heaping ¹/₂ cup caster (superfine) sugar
150 ml/5 fl oz/²/₃ cup water
2 egg yolks
125 g/4 oz/²/₃ cup chopped plain (bittersweet) chocolate, melted
125 g/4 oz/¹/₂ cup soft unsalted butter
icing (confectioners') sugar for dusting

Set the oven to 200°C/400°F/Gas 6 and line a greased 23 x 32 cm/9 x 13 inch Swiss roll tin (jelly roll pan) with greased greaseproof (waxed) or non-stick paper.

First make the buttercream. Boil the sugar and water for 5 minutes. Meanwhile, whisk the egg yolks, then pour in the sugar mixture and whisk well; add the chocolate, then gradually whisk in the butter. Chill, then whip before using.

To make the cake, whisk the eggs and sugar together in a bowl set over a pan of simmering water until they are pale and fluffy. Remove from the heat and stir in the cocoa. Whisk the egg whites until stiff, then fold these gently into the mixture.

Pour the mixture into the prepared tin (pan), spreading it out to the edges. Bake for 15 minutes. Cool the cake in the tin (pan) for 10 minutes, then cover with a damp cloth and leave for a further 10 minutes. Remove the cloth and turn the cake out on to a piece of greaseproof (waxed) paper that has been dusted with icing (confectioners') sugar. Remove the paper from the top of the cake and leave to cool completely.

When the cake is cold, trim the edges and spread the top with the whipped buttercream, then carefully roll the cake up from one of the long sides, using the paper to help: don't worry if it cracks. Sprinkle with more icing (confectioners') sugar. This log will keep well in the fridge, and can also be frozen successfully.

crunchy biscuit slices

To make coarse biscuit (cookie) crumbs, put them in a strong plastic bag and crush them with a rolling pin.

Line a Swiss roll tin (jelly roll pan) with non-stick paper. Put the butter into a heavy-based saucepan with the syrup and half the chopped chocolate. Heat gently until everything has melted.

Add the crushed biscuits (cookies) to the chocolate mixture and mix well until they are all coated. Spoon the mixture into the tin (pan) and press it down with the back of a spoon.

Melt the rest of the chocolate in a bowl over a pan of simmering water and spread over the top of the mixture. Leave until cold and set, then cut into serving pieces.

makes 24

50 g/2 oz/¼ cup butter
50 g/2 oz/2 tbsp golden
syrup (or light corn syrup)
200 g/7 oz/heaping 1 cup
chopped plain
(bittersweet) chocolate
200 g/7 oz/scant 1 cup
coarsely crushed plain
biscuits

swedish ring cake

This makes a pleasant change from the rich and spicy food of Christmas, while still looking festive. It is also, for some reason I've never quite been able to understand, extremely popular with children. They might prefer it without the cinnamon – mine certainly do.

makes one 20 cm/ 8 inch ring

75 g/3 oz/6 tbsp butter
³/₄ tsp sugar
³/₄ tsp salt
200 ml/7 fl oz/scant 1 cup milk and boiling water, mixed
350 g/12 oz/2¹/₂ cups strong white bread flour
1 sachet (package) easy-blend (rapid-rise) dried yeast
a little oil
50 g/2 oz/heaping ¹/₄ cup demerara sugar
1 tsp cinnamon – optional

for the glacé icing:
225 g/8 oz/heaping 1¹/₂ cups icing (confectioners') sugar
squeeze of lemon juice

to decorate:
red and green glacé (candied) cherries

Melt the butter without browning it, and leave to cool. Add the sugar and salt to the milk and water mixture, and stir until they have dissolved. Put the flour into a large bowl and sprinkle in the yeast. Make a well in the middle. When the melted butter is tepid, pour this into the well, along with most of the milk and water mixture, which should also be tepid: too hot and it will kill the yeast, too cold, and it will take ages to work. Mix the flour into the liquid, adding the rest as necessary, until you have a sticky dough.

Now, either turn the dough out on to a lightly floured surface and knead it for 10 minutes, or divide it into batches and process it in a food processor with the dough blade for 1 minute. In either case, it's ready when it's smooth and has lost its stickiness. It should still be fairly soft. Oil the base of your mixing bowl, put the ball of dough into this, then turn it up the other way so that the oily side is on top, to prevent a skin forming.

Put the bowl in a large plastic bag, closing it to exclude draughts, then leave it in a warm place. I generally stand it on a folded towel on a radiator and sometimes wrap a thick towel around it, too. Leave it for 1–2 hours, or until it has literally doubled in bulk.

Turn the risen dough out on to a lightly floured surface and knead it very briefly. Now press the dough out into a large rectangle, about 40 cm/16 inches long and 20 cm/8 inches across. Sprinkle the surface with the demerara sugar and the cinnamon if you're using this, then roll it up from one of the long sides and press the ends together to make a circle.

Place the ring on a baking sheet then, with scissors, make slanting cuts in the outer edge. Put the baking sheet inside the plastic bag again – or two bags if it's large – and leave in a warm place for a further ¾–2 hours, or until the ring is very fat and puffy. It's really important to let it rise enough, then you'll get a lovely light, springy cake.

About 20 minutes before you think this stage is reached, set the oven to 190°C/375°F/Gas 5. Bake the cake for 30–35 minutes, then remove from the oven and set aside to cool on a wire rack, with a cloth over it to soften the crust.

Make the icing by mixing the icing (confectioners') sugar with a squeeze of lemon juice and enough cold water to make a thick, just-spreadable consistency. Spread this over the top of the cake, and decorate with slices of red and green glacé (candied) cherries.

jean's cookies

makes 24

125 g/4 oz/$^1/_2$ cup soft margarine

50 g/2 oz/heaping $^1/_4$ cup caster (superfine) sugar

125 g/4 oz/1$^1/_3$ cups porridge (rolled) oats

25 g/1 oz/3 tbsp plain (all-purpose) flour

25 g/1 oz/3 tbsp semolina

25 g/1 oz/2 tbsp desiccated (shredded) coconut

$^1/_2$ tsp bicarbonate of soda (baking soda)

175–225 g/6–8 oz/1–1$^1/_3$ cups chopped chocolate, melted – optional

Set the oven to 140°C/275°F/Gas 1.

Put the margarine and sugar into a bowl and beat until creamy, then beat in all the other ingredients, except the chocolate, to make a stiff dough. On a lightly floured board, roll out the dough as thin as you can. If you find it too crumbly to work, add a drop or two of water, but don't over-do it. Stamp into rounds with a cutter and lift on to a baking sheet – they'll hardly spread at all, so can be quite close together.

Bake for 20 minutes. Let them cool on the sheet until you can handle them then, if you wish, dip each one in melted chocolate to half-coat it on the front and back. Leave on a wire rack to finish cooling and let the chocolate set.

peppermint stars

An easy recipe which children enjoy making, or helping to make. For a rather more elaborate version, the stars can be half-dipped in melted chocolate.

Put the egg white into a large bowl and whisk until it is frothy and well broken up. Sift in about half of the sugar and beat until smooth; continue in this way until you have a stiff, creamy mixture, and all, or nearly all, the sugar has been used. You may find it easier to use your hands to knead in the sugar as the mixture gets thick.

Flavour the mixture with a few drops of peppermint oil, then sift some sugar over a board and roll out the mixture quite thinly – to about 5 mm/¼ inch and cut into stars with a small cutter. Decorate each star with some silver balls, to make sparkly stars, if you wish, then put the stars on to a baking sheet lined with non-stick paper and leave them near a radiator or in a warm kitchen for a day or so until they have dried out.

Pack them into pretty boxes or in twists of coloured cellophane.

makes 30–40

1 egg white
350 g/12 oz/scant 2½ cups
icing (confectioners') sugar
plus extra for rolling out
a few drops of oil of
peppermint
silver balls – optional

christmas flowers

This is a great favourite with my family, particularly the girls. The 'flowers' are crisp biscuits moulded into shape over a small cup while they are still warm. The goodies inside can be as plain or as partified as you like.

makes 8

25 g/1 oz/2 tbsp butter
50 g/2 oz/scant ½ cup icing (confectioners') sugar, plus extra for dusting
25 g/1 oz/3 tbsp plain (all-purpose) flour
2–3 tbsp double (heavy) cream
1 egg white

for the filling:
vanilla ice cream
whipped double (heavy) cream
sweets (candies)
seedless grapes, raspberries, blueberries, nectarines, etc

Set the oven to 200°C/400°F/Gas 6. Draw four 10 cm/4 inch circles on a sheet of non-stick paper to fit a baking sheet.

Melt the butter, then mix it in with the sugar, flour, cream and egg white, beating well to make a smooth batter. Put a teaspoonful of this mixture on one of the circles, and spread it out carefully to cover the circle thinly. Make three more in the same way, then bake them for about 5 minutes, or until they are lightly browned. Set the unused mixture aside.

Have ready four small cups or jars the size of mustard jars. Lift the baked rounds off the paper and on to the inverted cups or jars, pressing the top to flatten it – this will be the base of the flower and needs to be level so that it will stand well. Curve the edges round the cup or jar to shape. Leave to cool, then remove. While the first lot are cooling, make more in the same way. These will keep for a day or two in an airtight tin, or carefully packed in a rigid container in the freezer.

To complete the flowers, stand them on a serving plate or on individual plates, and fill with tiny scoops of vanilla ice cream – a melon-bailer is good for making these – lightly whipped cream and some little sweets (candies) or pieces of fruit.

brandy snaps

Everyone loves brandy snaps, and they're surprisingly easy to make. They harden as they cool, so the trick is to lift them off the paper as soon as they're firm enough to handle, but before they get too brittle to roll – so keep testing them. If they do get too hard, just pop them back in the oven for a few seconds to soften them up again. You can fill them with cream or ice cream, or serve them plain, with a creamy fool, fruit compôte or sorbet.

Set the oven to 200°C/400°F/Gas 6. Line a large baking sheet with non-stick paper.

Put the syrup into a saucepan with the sugar and butter and melt over a gentle heat. Take the pan off the heat and stir in the flour, ground ginger and lemon juice.

Put heaped teaspoons of the mixture well apart on the baking sheet – you'll probably need to do at least two batches. Bake for 4–6 minutes, or until the brandy snaps are an even mid-golden brown, then remove from the oven and leave to cool on the paper for 2–3 minutes.

As soon as the brandy snaps are firm enough to pick up with a fish slice (wide metal spatula), lift them off the paper and mould each around the handle of a wooden spoon, or some other suitable cylinder shape. When the brandy snaps are cool and crisp, remove them and keep them in an airtight tin until you need them. To serve them, fill with cream which has been whipped with a little brandy, or with vanilla ice cream.

makes 12

50 g/2 oz/2 tbsp golden syrup (or light corn syrup)
50 g/2 oz/heaping ¹/₄ cup caster (superfine) sugar
50 g/2 oz/¹/₄ cup butter
50 g/2 oz/6 tbsp plain (all-purpose) flour
1 tsp ground ginger
1 tsp lemon juice

cinnamon shortbreads

These cinnamon shortbreads are delicious with Chocolate Ice Cream (page 157) or Christmas Dried Fruit Salad (page 143), as well as being good on their own, with tea or coffee.

makes 24

125 g/4 oz/³/₄ cup + 2 tbsp plain wholewheat flour
125 g/4 oz/³/₄ cup + 2 tbsp plain white (all-purpose) flour
50 g/2 oz/scant ¹/₂ cup cornflour (cornstarch)
50 g/2 oz/¹/₃ cup semolina or ground rice
2–3 tsp ground cinnamon
225 g/8 oz/1 cup soft butter
125 g/4 oz/heaping ¹/₂ cup caster (superfine) sugar

Set the oven to 170°C/325°F/Gas 3. Grease a 19 cm x 29 cm/7¹/₂ x 1¹/₂ inch shallow cake tin (pan) with butter.

Sift the flours, semolina or ground rice and the cinnamon into a large bowl or food processor adding the residue of bran from the sieve (strainer). Then put in the butter and the sugar. Whizz, or beat, all the ingredients together until they form a soft dough which leaves the sides of the bowl clean.

Press this into the prepared tin (pan), levelling the surface by pressing with the back of a metal spoon. Then prick the surface all over with a fork. Bake for about 45 minutes, until the shortbread is set and quite crisp on top and very lightly tinged with gold. It's more tricky to tell when these are done than with normal shortbreads because they are already rather brown. If you are in doubt, you can cut the shortbread and very carefully lift up one of the end pieces and look underneath it to see if it looks done. If not, carefully put it back and let the shortbread cook for a bit longer. When it's done, cut it into sections and leave it to cool and crisp up in the tin (pan).

This shortbread keeps well in an airtight tin for several days, if it gets the chance, and also freezes well. It thaws very quickly; you can use it almost straight from the freezer.

greek shortbreads

These make lovely petits fours, or, prettily packed, an attractive gift. Once they have been coated with rose water and icing sugar and then dried, they keep very well. Rose water is sold in most supermarkets, but if you cannot get it there, you will be sure to find it at a Middle Eastern store.

Set the oven to 170°C/325°F/Gas 3. Line 2 large baking sheets with non-stick paper.

Put the butter and sugar into a bowl or food processor and whizz, or beat, them together until they are light, then beat in the egg yolk. Sift the flour and cornflour (cornstarch) into the bowl, add the ground almonds, and mix gently until everything is combined.

Break off small pieces of the dough, about the size of a marble, and form them into crescents or barrel shapes. Put them on to the baking sheets, leaving a little space around them: they will expand a bit, but not too much. Bake for about 25 minutes, or until they are set but not coloured. Cool on a wire rack.

When the shortbreads are cool, put 6 tbsp rose water into a small bowl and sift the icing (confectioners') sugar into another bowl. Dip each shortbread quickly first into the rose water, then into the sugar. Return them to the wire rack and leave in a warm room for several hours. Pack them in a tin, or in boxes, sprinkling extra icing (confectioners') sugar between the layers, and on top.

225 g/8 oz/1 cup soft butter
50 g/2 oz/ heaping ¼ cup caster (superfine) sugar
1 egg yolk
275 g/10 oz/2 cups plain (all-purpose) flour
50 g/2 oz/scant ½ cup cornflour (cornstarch)
90 g/3½ oz/heaping 1 cup ground almonds
about 6 tbsp triple-distilled rose water
350–450 g/12 oz– 1 lb/2½–3 cups icing (confectioners') sugar

VEGAN VERSION
Just leave out the egg yolk, and use a vegan margarine instead of the butter.

mini florentines

makes about 60

50 g/2 oz/¹/₄ cup butter
50 g/2 oz/4 tbsp caster
(superfine) sugar
50 g/2 oz/¹/₃ cup glacé
(candied) cherries, finely
chopped
75 g/3 oz/heaping ¹/₂ cup
hazelnuts, finely chopped
25 g/1 oz/3 tbsp mixed
peel, finely chopped
2 tsp lemon juice
100 g/4 oz/²/₃ cup chopped
chocolate, half plain
(bittersweet) and half
white

Melt the butter in a saucepan, then add the sugar and bring to the boil, stirring all the time. Remove from the heat and stir in the cherries, hazelnuts, peel and lemon juice. Allow to cool slightly while you line 2 baking sheets with non-stick paper.

Set the oven to 180°C/350°F/Gas 4.

Put little heaps of the mixture, about the size of a hazelnut, on the sheets, leaving room for them to spread. Bake for 5–6 minutes, until they are a light golden brown. Push the edges in with a knife to neaten, then leave them to cool on the paper.

Melt the chocolate in 2 separate bowls set over saucepans of simmering water, or in a microwave for 3–4 minutes, then spread over the smooth side of the florentines. Just before the chocolate sets, make wavy lines with a fork. Leave to cool completely.

macaroons

Set the oven to 180°C/350°F/Gas 4 and line a baking
sheet with non-stick paper.

Put the ground almonds into a bowl with the sugar and
almond extract, then mix in enough of the egg white to
make a stiff mixture. You may not need all the egg white.
Either put teaspoonfuls of the mixture well apart on the
baking sheet, or pipe small mounds, using a piping bag
with a 1 cm/½ inch plain nozzle (tip), allowing room to
spread. Sprinkle with sugar and top with half an almond.

Bake for 15–20 minutes, or until set and golden brown.
Allow to firm up on the paper, then lift off on to a wire
rack to finish cooling.

makes 12–14

**125 g/4 oz/1⅓ cups ground
almonds**
**175 g/6 oz/scant 1 cup
caster sugar**
**a few drops of almond
extract**
**2 egg whites, lightly
whisked**
granulated sugar
**6–7 almonds, blanched and
halved**

stained glass windows

makes about 24

75 g/3 oz/$^1/_2$ cup + 2 tbsp
plain white (all-purpose)
flour
75 g/3 oz/$^1/_2$ cup + 2 tbsp
wholewheat flour
125 g/4 oz/$^1/_2$ cup butter
40 g/1$^1/_2$ oz/3 tbsp icing
(confectioners') sugar
about 24 boiled sweets
(candies) of different
colours: red, orange, green,
yellow and purple

Set the oven to 180°C/350°F/Gas 4 and line 2 large baking sheets with non-stick paper.

Beat together the flours, butter and sugar to make a dough. On a lightly floured board, roll out the dough to a depth of 2.5 mm/1 inch. Cut out shapes which are large enough to take a sweet (candy) in the middle, allowing for it to spread a bit. Then cut a circle out of the middle of the biscuits, about the size that the sweet (candy) will spread to. I use the round end of a piping nozzle (tip) for this. Put the biscuits on the baking sheets – they won't spread much – and pop a sweet (candy) into the middle of each.

Bake for about 10 minutes, or until the sweets (candies) have melted and the biscuits look golden brown, set and are browning a little more at the edges. Leave to cool on the sheets, but before they get completely firm, make a little hole in the top of each, well away from the edges, through which you can thread some cord to hang them on the tree.

index